The Love of God in the Classroom.

The story of the new Christian Schools

The Love of
God in the Classroom.

The story of the new Christian Schools

Sylvia Baker and
David Freeman

CHRISTIAN FOCUS

Contents

Acknowledgements

We are very grateful to William Mackenzie of Christian Focus Publications whose support for the concept of this book has so encouraged us.

Many others have also helped us. In particular, we would like to thank Monica Stringer and also the head teachers of the seventeen schools.

Finally, we want to thank all those who, in responding to God's call, have worked, sacrificed and prayed to bring about the new schools whose success is the subject of this book.

Foreword

This book offers a very personal, detailed account of the remarkable development of a new generation of Christian schools in the United Kingdom. It focuses on their amazing growth as they have mushroomed during the last 20 or so years on the initiative of local Christian communities. Dismayed by what they perceive as poor academic and behavioural standards in their local state schools, many parents, teachers and churches have made great personal and financial sacrifices to establish these, their own independent schools

I can personally testify to the achievements – spiritual, personal and academic – of those new Christian schools which I have visited. They include the King's School at Witney, the River School in Worcester and the Christian School in Nottingham. I was always impressed first and foremost by the ethos: these were places where children were manifestly happy. There was no sense at all of intimidation associated with bullying or aggressive behaviour. The children were enjoying lessons in an atmosphere of personal engagement with teachers, who clearly cared for them as individuals and were keen to help them on a personal one-to-one basis. Although in some cases, the physical facilities could not compare favourably with a local-authority funded school nearby, great efforts were made to give the children an all-round education and the results speak for themselves!

My first encounter with such a school is not included in the book, but I will never forget the lesson it taught me. The John Loughborough School was developed by the Seventh Day Adventist church, with considerable financial sacrifice from a community, which was far from wealthy, in a deprived part of North London. When I had the privilege of participating in one of their Awards Ceremonies in the 1980s, I remember a Governor happily telling me: "We no longer have to send our children 3000 miles away back home to get a good, old-fashioned, Christian, traditional British education. We can now have this here in London." Quoting this later in a debate in the House of Lords, I pointed out that it should not have been necessary for that community to send their children back to the West Indies for an education which should have been their birthright in this country.

The book describes in detail the experiences encountered by many parents and teachers who have had similar concerns to those of the John Loughborough School. Deeply committed to ensuring that their children receive an education compatible with the fundamental beliefs, values and principles of behaviour which they try to instil at home, they faced the innumerable challenges of starting up their own schools. The stories recount different and formidable problems of establishing new Christian schools in many parts of the country – from Southampton and Plymouth in the South and South-West, Witney and Worcester in 'middle-England', Liverpool, Cheshire and Sheffield further north, to the far-flung Scottish Isle of Lewis and across the Irish Sea to Bangor in Northern Ireland.

Written in a very homely and intimate style, the book is an 'easy-read'. Each new school is a remarkable story of vision, faith, courage, sacrifice, commitment – and, ultimately, success! Each school also faced crises and challenges and there are many 'miracles' – if, by 'miracle' one includes events of responses to prayer of such amazing timing and precision that it seems that only a divine intervention could have been at work! These stories are therefore not only an account of a remarkable series of achievements in educational terms, but a source of inspiration and a challenge to all Christians to remember the power of prayer. They also challenge us to remember God's faithfulness: if we are willing to seek His will and to step out in faith with Him, He can do more than we could ever imagine.

As someone who shares the Christian faith, I could be accused of bias and partiality. It is very important therefore to look at independent evaluations and indices of success. I was very pleased and reassured to read the positive reports by independent School Inspectors in Ofsted inspections. I have also always been concerned about criticisms I have heard made by many people about issues such as whether pupils from such 'protected' environments would be at a disadvantage when they encountered the challenges of the wider world or whether they would be able to make effective contributions in more heterogeneous communities, such as the local Sixth Form or Tertiary Colleges they would later attend. Again, this book gives many reassuring testimonies of the ways in which school-leavers are appreciated in their subsequent schools or colleges. Similarly, there are reports of very positive evaluations by employers of graduates of these schools who appreciate the qualities they bring from the education they have received in these Christian schools.

Finally, there was always the concern over whether the pupils themselves would appreciate or resent the experience of attending one of these distinctive schools. The book abounds with positive testimonies from former students who, often while they are still pupils, and particularly in retrospect, emphasise how much they appreciate the education received.

Clearly, a sceptical reader might justifiably wonder whether the positive evaluations are typical – or whether they have been carefully selected and are not truly representative. However, having visited some of these schools, and having the privilege of knowing some of those who have become leaders of what has now become the Christian School Movement, I trust their integrity. The stories in this book ring true.

This country has, of course, many well-established faith-based schools such as those founded in the Anglican, Roman Catholic and Methodist denominations. They range from independent schools, some with historic and international reputations to many more locally-based, state-funded 'voluntary' or 'voluntary-aided' denominational schools. Such schools, founded in the Christian tradition have generally achieved widespread recognition for their levels of academic attainment and for their protection of fundamental spiritual and moral values, reflected in relatively high standards of behaviour, with fewer problems of truancy and anti-social behaviour than many of their secular counterparts with comparable catchment areas. They have therefore often proved popular with local parents and are often over-subscribed, attracting applications even from those who adhere to other religious faiths – or none.

Other religious traditions also have established their own schools: for example, there are a number of well-established Jewish schools and now other faith communities such as Muslims are enabled to follow suit.

Those who share the theological 'genre' of the authors of this book will find the style more conducive than some who come from different backgrounds. But I hope that it will be read by many people from broader and more diverse traditions, because its message is truly inspiring. It is essentially an account of what can be achieved by people of faith, motivated by love, who are prepared to listen to God and to respond in trust.

It is also a celebration of belief in our spiritual heritage and a commitment to ensuring that this heritage is preserved, protected and passed on to our children and our children's children. We who have inherited faith and freedom have the responsibility to pass on this legacy to the next generation – undiminished. Those whose endeavours are described in this book are trying to fulfil this mandate. I pray God will bless their endeavours – and, through them, His church and His people in this nation and far beyond.

Caroline Cox
(Baroness Cox)

Stornaway

Dundee

Edinburgh (2)

Dumfries

Bangor

Preston   Bradford
Wigan   Rochdale
      Bury   Barnsley
Liverpool   Stalybridge
Sale   Sheffield
Manchester   Stockport
Derby (2)   Ilkeston
             Dronfield
Walsall   Nottingham
         Leicester
      Worcester
   Gloucester
Witney (2)   Oxford
Bristol   Harpenden
         London (4)   Romford
Basingstoke
Winchester   Epsom
            Croydon (3)   Rochester
         Eastleigh
Southampton
Exeter
Plymouth

Introducing the New Christian Schools

For the past thirty years, almost unnoticed by the wider Christian community in the UK, a powerful movement has been developing across the nation. The leaders tend to be people that few have heard of. The movement has received very little financial backing from either the churches or the Government. It has been attended by a sense of great struggle and sacrifice, and has had to contend with opposition and verbal abuse. Yet the movement, in retrospect, can rightly be called powerful. There are now thousands of graduates of the new Christian schools. They are already beginning to make their mark on society. The hundred, or so, schools that are currently in existence are influences for good in the areas where they are situated. Much more has been accomplished than the early pioneers would ever have dreamt was possible.

The first stirrings

My own interest in Christian schooling began in the early seventies, when my husband I were both young teachers at secondary schools in the London area. The schools were commendable in many ways and had good reputations locally. Nevertheless, as time went by, we felt an increasing sense of unease. There was an ethos prevailing in the schools and it wasn't a Christian one. The underlying message coming through the education that we saw the young people receiving was that the main purpose of life was to get a good job and make money. We also saw them being trained to think of right and wrong as very relative terms. This was not at all the manner in which we wanted our own young children to be educated. We were working hard to instil Christian values into them at home. Did we really want all those values to be challenged as soon as they stepped into school? Could five year olds really cope with that? Would they not be more likely to absorb the values of the community into which we had sent them to be educated?

We were forced to consider what it really means to bring up a child in the fear of the Lord and to train that child to serve the Lord in today's world, loving him with all his or her heart, soul, mind and strength. We had to face the challenge of the following question: is it consistent with that command to send your child to be trained by someone who may not know the Lord and may even despise him and his truth?

Time to take action

By the time that our eldest child had reached school age, we had moved from London to the Manchester area. There we met up with a few other parents who felt the same way as we did – that the only way forward was to establish a Christian school. This seemed a very frightening prospect. We realised that, as a venture of faith, to take this step would put everything else that we had ever been involved with as Christians completely in the shade. We stepped forward – and it proved to be even more difficult than we had thought it would be! As we struggled with financial difficulties, general opposition and exhaustion, we began to suspect that we were right on the front line of the spiritual battle.

It was a very great privilege to be involved in the education of so many precious children and the issues and principles that we had only dimly recognised in the beginning began to come into much sharper focus. Soon we began to see that to teach children without specific reference to God's true place in everything would be to train them in godlessness. The Christian world view began to seem richer and richer once we were free to base all of our teaching on it. We saw, as well, more clearly than ever how radically different the whole area of character training and discipline is when conducted in a Christian context.

More schools
After a few years of feeling isolated and alone in this endeavour, we became dimly aware that there were other Christian schools springing up across the country. Soon we had had contact with some of them. What a very great encouragement it was to find that the Lord had led them along such similar paths to the one we had trodden. Independently of each other, we had come under the same deep convictions. We realised with a sense of awe that we were actually part of a movement that God had initiated.

More benefits
With the benefit of hindsight, it can now be seen that the new Christian schools' movement has actually accomplished more than just the education of thousands of children. That of course has been its main aim and focus, but there have been some unexpected side benefits. For one thing, the Christian schools have proved to be places where many people have found Christ for the first time, both children and adults. It was

not very long before our own school began to be approached by non-Christian families, wanting the high standards that they perceived us to be offering. Soon we were hearing of conversion experiences. It seemed that people had been able to see Christianity at work; the Gospel had somehow been made visible through what we were doing. The other Christian schools report exactly the same thing.

The Christian schools have also been forces for good in their neighbourhoods in that they have often been able to help families with needy children, for whom the other schools are not working for one reason or another. Often what is needed is the loving atmosphere that a Christian school is uniquely able to provide. What better environment for any child than one where the love of Christ is known and felt? The Christian schools are well aware that they are not perfect institutions and that they have made many mistakes. Nevertheless, the Lord Jesus promised that, where his people were meeting in his name, he would be present in a special way and that is the testimony of the schools and of those who visit them.

Another unexpected side-effect of the establishment of Christian schools is a most astonishing one. Christians of different theological persuasions have actually been able to work together, side by side, day after day, year after year, without falling out!

Although some of the schools are linked to specific churches, others are parent cooperatives or founded by groups of churches. It is not uncommon to find the complete range of Christian theology and experience represented in a school. The task at hand is so important that everyone involved focuses on the central issues; secondary issues become just that.

Has it worked?
In 2001, I began to conduct some research in an effort to find

out how our past pupils felt about the schooling that they had received. Had the dire predictions of those who had opposed us been fulfilled? Had we produced a generation of poorly educated, narrow and bigoted individuals who had unhappy memories of their school days and who had not been able to cope with the real world? I sent out questionnaires to as many former pupils as I could track down. The 65 responses that I received exceeded my wildest dreams. I did of course know that they were not poorly educated; the great majority had left our school with excellent GCSE results, often well above the levels that their cognitive abilities would have predicted them for. I was more interested in what they had made of their lives since they left and here I was far from disappointed. They seemed to be the opposite of narrow and bigoted. They seemed well adjusted and to be successfully pursuing worthwhile careers. Best of all, their memories were of happy school days, full of love and good relationships.

That research has now been extended to other Christian schools, with very similar results. To date, we have received a total of 240 responses from eleven different schools.

Even allowing for the possibility that those who have returned questionnaires are the ones who are most positive about their schooling, the results are very encouraging.

Of the 240 young adults, aged between 17 and 32, who returned their questionnaires, 80% describe themselves as practising Christians. 73% are members of churches. 70% did not feel that they had been in any way over protected and 78% felt well prepared for the next stage of life. A resounding 87% said unreservedly that they had enjoyed their time at school. When asked to comment on their memories of their school days, over and over again the young people spoke of a loving environment where they enjoyed good relationships with both fellow pupils and with staff.

Of course, the schools are not perfect places and they are constantly aiming to improve, striving to learn to be more Christ-like and to deal with any weaknesses as they become apparent. However, there is no doubt at all that they have been successful in producing well-educated, well-rounded individuals who increasingly appreciate and value the nature of the schooling that they received. The schools have achieved this against tremendous odds and with far fewer resources than would be available in the state system, let alone in most of the private sector. It has taken much sacrifice on the part of parents and teachers and has been accompanied by earnest prayer. What has been demonstrated beyond question is the positive benefit of an education that places the Lord Jesus Christ at the centre.

It has been my very great privilege to compile the material that follows. When I started researching the stories of the schools, I thought I already knew quite a lot about them. I soon realised my mistake. I had had no idea that so many miracles had taken place, that so many major steps of faith had been taken by individuals here in the UK at the end of the 20th century.

Read on. You will be astonished.

Sylvia Baker
August 2004

1

How it all began

The Cedars School, Rochester

The very first of the new Christian schools opened in Rochester in 1969. Several years earlier than the next one that we know of, and when 99.9% of the church in the UK was content to leave the education of children to others, a group of Christians were given the faith to step out on their own. This is their amazing story.

A mother's vision
The opening of The Cedars, the very first of the new Christian schools, came about through the faith and obedience of Betty Harris, a mother of five children. In the mid sixties, Betty was guided by the Lord to begin to train as a teacher and also to take over the running of a nursery school. She then began to feel strongly that God was calling her to provide children with a Christ-centred education. One day, she received a vision from the Lord in which she saw little children with hands outstretched, yearning for something. The Lord said to her, 'Where are the people who will feed my children with the Living Bread?' It became very clear to her that the Lord wanted

a Christ-centred school in Rochester, even though such a thing was unknown in Britain at the time.

While Betty was running her nursery school, it had begun to seem very strange to her that Christians should put such young children into the alien environment of a secular school where the standards and ethos would be so very different from their homes. Surely at such a very impressionable age, they should be being trained in the Lord's ways. Betty had seen how children soak up everything that is given to them, like sponges! She had also seen, through her own children and through running the nursery school, how open young children are to receive from the Lord.

The Bible speaks

The Lord spoke to Betty through many Bible verses of the responsibility given to Christian parents to bring up their own children in the training and discipline of the Lord. She became convinced that a school should be started to help believing parents to fulfil these commands. These same convictions would, ten or so years later, begin to affect other groups of Christians in just the same way, but in the mid sixties, it seemed that Betty and her husband Arthur were lone pioneers.

The hunt is on!

In 1968, Betty and Arthur began to look for a building for a school. One day, Betty felt that the Lord was urging her to go to look at a certain building. It had been in use for many years as an independent school for young children but that school was now closing and the building was coming up for sale. A Christian surveyor came along too, having kindly agreed to survey the property without charging a fee. While they were in the building, they began to talk to an elderly lady who had been in the school's employment for many years. She was in real spiritual and physical need and Betty and the surveyor were able to speak to her about the Lord Jesus. The surveyor examined the property very carefully and they left feeling encouraged that the Lord had led them there that day.

A few days later, the surveyor contacted Betty to say that, after prayer, he no longer felt that this was the right building for the proposed Christian school, mainly because of its position, which would give them no room to expand. However, he felt that the Lord had given him two verses for Betty. They were Matthew 19:21, *'Sell all that you have and you shall have treasure in Heaven.'* Together with Psalm 18:29, *'By my God, I have leapt over a wall.'* Betty and Arthur and their prayer group, having weighed this up before the Lord, agreed that the surveyor was right.

The Lord speaks
Betty now needed to return to the house to explain that they no longer intended to proceed with the purchase. As she left the building and went out of the gate, she talked to the Lord, voicing how puzzled she felt about what had happened. 'Why should the surveyor have spent all that time doing a thorough survey that you, Lord, knew wasn't going to be needed?' Straight away the reply came.

'Because there was someone in the house that day who needed me. I want you to learn from this that each child is precious in my eyes and that no trouble is to be spared in the training of my children, in prayer and in the care that I am asking you to give them.'

'Thank you, Lord,' said Betty, 'and what shall I do now?'

Immediately, the name of an estate agent came into Betty's mind. On going to see him, she explained what she wanted. It felt as though the estate agent had been expecting her. He listened carefully, and then said, 'Here is the key to just the sort of place you need for a school.'

The place was ideal; the snag was that there was no money available! The Lord again spoke clearly to Betty and Arthur and those praying with them. In a marvellous way he opened up his purpose for the future and revealed to them that they would eventually have a full age range in the school. He also made it clear that they should rely on him as their Heavenly Father and be obedient to him in the matter of finance. They were to receive no grants or government funding. They were not to ask for money from anyone nor were they to let it be known that they were in need. An exciting time followed as they watched and prayed. Sure enough, the money for the building arrived and The Cedars School was able to begin.

A very unusual school

From its very beginning, The Cedars has been a very unusual school. It was as though the Lord was calling this school to pioneer Christian schooling in a most radical way. He made it clear that they were to charge no fees and pay no salaries. They were to rely on the Lord to prompt people to give donations. A gift given a few years after they began enabled them to buy another house to accommodate full-time staff and they were therefore able to form their first community. Full-time staff were to receive no salaries, but would be provided with food and accommodation. The school is still run in this way today. The residential community is augmented by part-time staff and parents who provide many different kinds of help.

Why did they pick the name 'The Cedars' for the school? Inspiration for this came from Psalm 92:12. '*The godly will flourish like palm trees and grow strong like the cedars of Lebanon.*' The school considers that the children themselves are the cedars, growing up in the presence of the Lord.

The Lord speaks again

In 1971, the Holy Spirit spoke to Betty in a special way. Through the study of God's word, and through prayer, she became convinced that the council properties that surrounded them would eventually belong to the school as well. One was next door, the Rates Office. A very large Victorian building, right opposite, was the Surveyors' Department. Within its grounds there was a bungalow, an old coach house and a temporary office building. One Sunday, Betty was standing at her window looking out at these buildings. She was meditating on a verse from the Bible that had been read in church that morning. Isaiah 42:9 says, *'See, the former things have taken place, and the new things I declare; before they spring into being I announce them to you'* (NIV). Opposite the window was the Surveyors' Department and Betty suddenly realised that the long damson hedge in front of it was in nearly full bloom even though it was only January! Clearly and powerfully into her mind came a word from the Lord, 'You shall have this place and the others.' The impression was so strong that it was almost as though she had heard an audible voice.

At the time, to be able to acquire such buildings seemed like an impossible dream, but Betty told the children, parents, staff and friends what she believed the Lord had said. For nine years, the school community watched and waited for this promise to be fulfilled. One building did become vacant, but when they asked the council if they could buy it, they were told that it would be pulled down for redevelopment. They went back to the Lord but his answer to them was the same: 'You shall have it.' Throughout the nine years, the Lord encouraged them again and again, with Bible verses, pictures and words from the Lord, especially from the children. Eventually, a new council was elected, and the school made another offer for the vacant building. This time they were told that the buildings were for sale and so negotiations began. Difficulties were encountered which dragged on for months and felt most unpleasant, but during this time the other council buildings also became available. Eventually, the council decided to put the three large buildings up for auction in April 1980. One plot contained a bungalow and an office unit as well.

Costly faith

The night before the auction, the Lord spoke to Arthur and said, 'You are to buy all three of the buildings whatever the cost.' That same evening, a gift came through the letter box and they added it to their existing funds. The total amount would be all that they had to offer as a deposit the next day. A deposit of 10% would be required, but 10% of how much? Would what they had be enough? The next day the buildings sold for £211,000 and the deposit they had available came to exactly 10% of this!

The sale of the buildings was reported in the local paper under the heading '**Religious group has month to raise the money for properties**'.

A religious group which successfully bid £211,000 for properties in Rochester at a big auction last week has now admitted that it does not have the money to pay for them. But representatives of the Cedar Foundation maintain that it will raise the money within the required month.

Trial of faith

The most testing time followed this initial victory. One month passed and then two but, thankfully, each time the deadline was extended. Many donations came in. One man from the market gave £1,000 in notes as a thanksgiving because he had come back to faith in Christ. The children were very much involved in praying for the finance. One small boy told Betty that he believed that when she came downstairs during the night, she would find some money on the doormat. That night Betty was bombarded by doubt about the whole situation and got up to pray. Peace returned to her heart and she went to check on the doormat. There was a cheque for £100! Although it was a relatively small amount it was a sign that God had not forgotten them. One little girl, whose parents were not even Christians, insisted that they should read the story of the feeding of the 5,000. The next day she came to school and said they should read it again, so Betty asked the Lord what he wanted them to hear from it. It seemed that the Lord wanted the children to give. They brought their pennies and gave them towards the costs of the buildings. Together these amounted to about £5.00. Soon a gift of £5,000 was received from previous parents who knew nothing about the current needs of The Cedars! It was as though the Lord had multiplied the children's giving a thousand times!

Before the auction, a little boy came into school on a Monday morning saying that he had had a 'word from Jesus' over the weekend from the book of Ezra saying, ' All expenses will be paid by the king'. The prayers of the children counted; they were very much a part of the story of pioneering the school.

The donations continued to flood in, some small and other larger amounts. The whole matter had received much coverage by the local press, so many people knew about it. Finally, after three months the total amount was received. The local press had a field day. One newspaper reported,

'A religious charity in Medway has performed a miracle and raised the £190,000 it desperately needed in just 4 months. And today they described the incredible feat as a "triumph of faith". Hundreds of donations from all over the world have rewarded that faith. People who couldn't afford cash gave personal items like small pieces of jewellery. The foundation are to have a Thanksgiving Service when the school resumes in September. (This took place in Rochester Cathedral.) Headmistress Mrs. Betty Harris said, 'We have never asked for money, it has just come. The children have never doubted that the money would be raised. At their morning "Praise Time" the children have been reading texts saying that the buildings would be bought.'

Another paper had the headlines, '**Foundation's £200,000 is gift from "Bank of Heaven".**' The Chatham Standard showed a photo of Betty and Arthur being handed the keys to the buildings.

The Cedars today

The school continues, down to the present day, to trust in the Lord and to see his provision. The original building has now been sold for £270,000 and the school brought together on one site of about one acre. The facilities include a tarmaced playground, a separate nursery building, a block for the junior school and a large rambling house called the 'Ark' for the seniors. The old coach house has been turned into an assembly room and there are two ponds for nature studies. This is certainly evidence that God supplies the needs of his children! The school is well equipped with a science lab, a kitchen for cookery and a room where they can learn about textiles. They use the grounds for scientific investigation and gardening, and local facilities for sports. From a young age the children are involved in art, craft, design, technology, drama and music. They have swimming lessons, tennis, football, cricket, hockey, netball and ice-skating.

Although the early pioneering days are past, it is still necessary to trust the Lord and to seek him for all their needs. A more recent prayer project was the re-surfacing of the playground. Again, this need was made known to the Lord in prayer together with the children. The faith of the little ones grew, and with it the anticipation of using their new playground. They brought their own small gifts from their pocket money and saw God multiply them.

The vision fulfilled

Initially, the school began with junior age children. Now, the children are aged 3-16 and take their GCSEs before leaving. A full range of subjects is covered throughout the school and every subject is taught from a Christ-centred perspective.

'God is the only absolute we have in our world of ever changing values,' says Betty. 'He is the only fixed reference point. Without him and his Word, the tides and fashions of history come and go and we are "all at sea" because everything is relative and unattached. It is essential for us all – both teachers and pupils – that we learn what pleases him lest we find ourselves an obstruction on his path.'

The school believes that creation reflects the character of the Creator. Because Jesus himself told his disciples to look at the flowers and at the birds, the children are taught to look at such things and to enjoy them. Betty believes that it is the heritage of children to be happy and to learn how to be happy with others. There is firm discipline in the school, administered within a loving atmosphere.

The highest priority

The greatest priority in the children's education is for them to come to know the Lord. As they grow older, they are taught to know him more fully as Saviour and Lord, Guide and Counsellor. The school believes that training the children in the ways of orderliness, obedience, forgiveness, kindness and love, within the context of a reverent fear of the Lord, brings a firm foundation for relationships, characterised by the knowledge and love of God. The great commission given by Jesus (Matt. 28:19, 20) to 'go and make disciples of all nations' is stressed in the school. There are opportunities for the students to pray, study the Bible and learn about missions and their world is further enriched by visiting speakers, many from different lands.

What are the results?

Inspectors have spoken very highly of the school. Betty remembers a visit in the early days. The very first time that an inspector came he spent all day and asked many questions. At the time the school only had junior children. On the basis of what he had seen the inspector said that he would like to see a senior school established. 'What concrete evidence do you have that you will have the means to do this?' he said.

'Only God's Word,' Betty replied, knowing that it was at God's request that the school had begun.

'Seriously,' the Inspector said, 'I should need some advice in reporting that to the Ministry of Education.'

The senior school has now been flourishing for over twenty years, and continues to be praised by school inspectors. In a much more recent report in October 2002, it was said, 'HMI is satisfied that the Cedars School is a secure community that is characterised by good relationships and a clear commitment to distinctive and firmly held religious principles. Pupils are happy at the school, are courteous and polite and behave well. The school provides a good foundation on which pupils can build for the future.'

This has been reflected in the good GCSE results obtained by the pupils over the years.

Former students have fitted in well in places of further study and employment. They have successfully gone on to sixth forms and universities, gaining a wide variety of qualifications and moving on to worthwhile careers. One of the most rewarding times is when ex-students return to the school with their interesting stories and express appreciation of the good foundation that the school gave them.

Betty considers it a great privilege to be involved in making known to God's people their specific inheritance concerning their children, believing that '*The kingdom of God belongs to such as these*' (Mark 10:14). She wishes that her own children could have had such an education, but is thrilled that nine of her grandchildren have attended the school.

In 1969, the Lord called The Cedars School into being to pioneer the first wave of new Christian schools. More than thirty years later, their visible success over such a long period is both a challenge and a great encouragement to the schools that have followed. They have proved the truth of one of their favourite verses, Psalm 127:1, which says, '*Unless the Lord builds a house, the work of the builders is useless.*'

Some parents comment:

'We want our children to receive the same moral teaching and the same understanding of the world in the home, in the church and in the school. We believe that the true basis for human relationships is found in the fact that we are all created in the image of God, that we have been given a series of moral absolutes and are accountable to Him for our actions.

We took the decision to remove our children from the State system after much thought and prayer. Although it has meant considerable sacrifice in terms of finance, travelling time and physical effort for our three children to attend The

Cedars School, we believe they are receiving an education for life.'

A pupil comments:
'A Christian school provides an environment that can be compared to a family. Some people accuse Christian schools of being soft, but the truth is they are loving and caring.'

In Christ lie hidden all the treasures of wisdom and knowledge (Col. 2:3).

2

An Impossible Dream Come True
Trinity School, Stalybridge, Cheshire

Small beginnings

Towards the end of January, 1978, a small group of parents met together to talk about the education of their children. The six sets of parents were all Christians and their children were very young. In their homes, they were bringing the little ones up to know and love God. They were teaching them the Bible and training them according to Christian principles. The problem that they had met to discuss was this. Would the local schools be able to continue to train their children in this way? Was it not much more likely that the children would receive a very different kind of education, one that was not based on Christian principles? Would it not be true that other views would shape the way the children were handled and influence the subject matter they were taught?

By the end of that evening, the twelve parents had come to a very radical decision. They would start a school of their own – one in which the Lord Jesus Christ would be central to everything that was taught, one that would reflect the Christian ethos and values of their own homes. In practical terms, it seemed an impossibility. Although some of them were teachers, they were all young, the average age being about 31. They had no experience of founding a school, no premises, no staff and very little money between them. All they had were a handful of small children and a powerful burden from God.

Opposition and heart-searching

The little group of parents did not know, first-hand, of any other venture in the whole of the United Kingdom like the one they were proposing. They did not have the support of a group of churches, or even of one church. Most church leaders that they approached seemed to be hostile to the idea of a Christian school. Indeed, right from the beginning, the founders of Trinity School encountered opposition from those who believed that they were making a big mistake. 'You will not be able to succeed,' they were told. 'You cannot possibly expect such an amateurish arrangement to achieve good examination results or preparation for future careers. The children will suffer. They will not be prepared for life in the real world. They will have been shielded too much from what life is really like. And anyway, children from Christian homes should be in secular schools to provide a Christian witness. The children from your school will emerge narrow-minded and bigoted from such a brainwashing as you are planning to give them. They will be socially inadequate and unable to relate well to others because of the narrow Christian ethos and because of the small numbers.'

The parents weighed all these criticisms very carefully. They asked themselves, 'What would constitute success? What would a well-educated child look like from God's point of view?'

Searching the Bible

They decided to look in the Bible for the answers to these questions and discovered a lot of relevant teaching. The Bible, they found, urges parents to teach their children God's ways, to bring them up in his training and instruction. It showed them that the fear of the Lord is the beginning of wisdom and that in Christ are hidden all the treasures of wisdom and knowledge.

The Bible stated quite plainly what God would require of them and their children. '*He has showed you, O people, what is good. And what does God require of you? To act justly and to love mercy and to walk humbly with your God*' (Micah 6:8). The more that the parents studied passages like these the less likely it seemed that such an education could be delivered by those who did not know God and who lived by quite a different code of conduct. They would have to move ahead with the plan for the school and leave the outcome in the hands of God himself.

The school begins

The plan was to open in September 1978 and to everyone's amazement that aim was achieved. On September 25th 1978, Trinity School opened its doors for the first time. The premises consisted of a large and pleasant outbuilding at the home of Bruce and Sylvia Baker in Mottram-in-Longdendale, Greater Manchester. Susan Ryan, another of the parents and an experienced primary teacher, had agreed to be the main teacher, teaching every morning, with several of the other mothers, one father and one grandmother covering the afternoons. On that first morning there were seven children in the school, aged between five and seven years. Soon another joined them. Those eight children and their parents were truly pioneers.

Temporary planning permission had been granted for a school of eight pupils to use the Mottram premises. At the end of the first year, the school governors confidently applied for that planning permission to be renewed. To their surprise, it was refused. It seemed that some of the neighbours had got up a petition, wanting the school to be closed. The local newspaper carried a dramatic headline, '**TRINITY SCHOOL MUST CLOSE. LOCAL PETITION HELPS TO SEAL ITS FATE.**' The anguished little school community gave themselves to prayer. Surely God would not let this happen! Was the fate of the school really sealed? Having had a year to see first-hand the benefits of a Christian education, most of the parents could not contemplate putting their children back into secular schools. However, having cried out to God, they received an unexpected answer.

A challenge from God

It seemed that God was saying to the tiny, fragile Christian school that He did want it to continue, but that He wanted it to be available to more children. Up to now, the parents had only been concerned about their own children. To educate just these seemed a big enough task. Now they were being urged to find bigger premises so that many more children could receive the benefits that only a Christian school could provide.

Once again, the small group of parents was forced to rely on God. How could they find alternative accommodation at such short notice? How could they finance it? The Mottram premises had been provided free of charge. How could such a small group of young parents take on an even bigger task? By now, the oldest children in the school were eight or nine years old and there were several four or five year olds waiting to join the youngest class. It had already been decided that two classes were now required, an infant class and a junior class. This would mean employing another teacher. Another salary and extra premises would now need to be paid for! It seemed impossible.

Much fervent prayer went up to God. What was the right thing to do? For some of the parents, there was no question about it. They could no longer bear to contemplate placing their children in an alien environment where their characters would be trained by those who did not know God and who had an entirely different outlook on life. Since God had given them such a strong burden about this, he could surely be trusted to provide the means to achieve it. Very quickly, new premises were found in the neighbouring town of Stalybridge. The school would be able to rent two small rooms and would have the use of some other facilities, in particular a large hall. So it was that in September 1979 Trinity School moved to Stalybridge and opened with two classes, an extra teacher, Christine Williamson, and eighteen children.

Financial pressures and answers to prayer
The first year had proved to be relatively easy to finance. The premises came free, as did much of the teaching, which was done on a voluntary basis. With the move to Stalybridge in 1979, a different situation was introduced. The budget was very much larger, but the parents did not want to charge fees. They did not want this precious Christian education to be restricted to those who had substantial means. God had told them to open their doors, to create extra space, to offer the benefits of this education much more widely and this they were now trying to do. Many years were to follow of financial struggle. How to raise the necessary finance became, and remains, a difficult issue. Trinity School was established on the principle that the education of children is primarily the responsibility of the parents. It has therefore always been the parent body that has given, worked, prayed and somehow survived the demands of financing the school for more than 25 years. In this they have been greatly helped by the sacrifices of the teachers, who have worked for very low salaries, and in some cases for no salary at all.

The need to continually pray for finance has resulted in some amazing stories of God's provision. Towards the end of 1979, the school community knew that they needed to pray hard if they were to cover their expenses for the year. One small pupil, six years old, was praying with his parents at bedtime. 'Please, God, send us £50 soon!' he asked. To him, this sounded a lot of money although the school actually needed much more. About an hour later, there was a ring at the doorbell. A friend of the family was standing there, holding out an envelope. 'God has told me to bring you this for the school.' he said, although he did not know that the school was in financial trouble. The envelope was found to contain exactly £50! Through experiences like these, the parents realised that God was training both them and their children to trust Him and to expect answers to prayer. At another time of crisis, when the school needed £12,000 to be able to balance its books that year, a parent re-mortgaged his house to raise that amount. On yet another occasion the school desperately needed £10,000. Through the letter box, at just the right time, came an anonymous gift for exactly that amount.

Two steps forward and ...
For two years, the fledgling Trinity School remained in the premises at Stalybridge. Numbers grew, and the children seemed to be developing well. However, very quickly a new challenge appeared on the horizon. The oldest children would soon reach secondary age. Would the school be able to cope with this? Again extra premises and extra staff would be needed. By now, the parent body was getting more used to taking steps of faith. In 1981, another move took place, this time to premises in nearby Gee Cross, Hyde. David and Pam Pott joined the staff and an extra senior class for secondary pupils was opened.

... one step back!

The school was now regarded as much more established, although in reality it was still very much a pioneering work. Over the next two or three years, numbers grew to around 50. However, the problem of finance remained. It seemed that there was never enough money to meet all the needs, even with so much voluntary help, and everything done on a shoestring. In early 1984, the situation became critical and radical steps were taken to remedy the situation. At the February half-term, the school closed, to open again two weeks later on a different footing. There were still no fees, but parents were asked for a higher level of commitment to the school. Numbers of children dropped back to about 35, but a time of greater stability for the school followed and the numbers soon began to grow again.

Every financial crisis led to an increase in prayer and a testing of the commitment of the parents. There were now many more than at the beginning who were deeply committed to wanting a Christian education for the children. This was not about an elite private education. The school was a humble institution with less than desirable facilities. It was about valuing the Christian ethos above everything else. It was about believing that this would provide the very best education for the children, better than anything that good facilities could provide without God. Had he not said , '*Those who honour me, I will honour*'? In those early days, this was very much a matter of faith. Today it can be seen to have been fulfilled in the outstandingly successful lives of so many Trinity graduates.

A permanent home at last

Soon after the crisis of 1984, the school was on the move again. This time, the opportunity had arisen for them to own their own building. In September 1985, Trinity School moved to a permanent site back in Stalybridge. This date coincided with another milestone. By now, those children who had been seven years old in 1978 were about to start Year 10. This is a new phase of education, when the exam courses begin, ready for public examinations two years later. In 1985, these were still O-level and CSE exams. The new GCSE was to be introduced one year later. The little school still suffered opposition from those who believed it could not possibly be doing a good job. Might not some of their criticisms be proved true if the school proceeded to the demands of examination-level education? At first it was decided that the school was not ready to take this step. There were, in any case, very few pupils of that age. At the last minute, in July, it was decided to try to proceed although at one point it looked as though there might only be one pupil in the O level class. More came forward over the summer and in the end, seven pupils took O level and CSE in the summer of 1987. The results were due out in the August, and were awaited with much trepidation. What excitement there was when it was realised that the candidates had done really well! The following year, the first group to sit GCSEs also did well and in 1989 the first cohort to have received all their schooling at Trinity achieved a very high standard indeed.

Groundless fears

It is now seventeen years since public exams were first taken at Trinity School and about 250 pupils have been involved in them. In 1993, the first league tables were published. As they are an independent school, Trinity did not at first realise that their results would be included. They were therefore taken by surprise when a reporter from a local newspaper phoned to get their reaction to the news that Trinity School had come top of the league in Tameside! This success has been repeated ever since; in the eleven years, to date, that league tables have been published, the school has always been in either first or second place.

The pupils, contrary to those early criticisms and fears, have achieved far above what they would have been expected to achieve if they had been in the state system. This has been verified using data published by the National Foundation for Educational Research which links a child's expected GCSE results to their results in cognitive ability tests. This gives an independent measure of how Trinity pupils have performed in GCSEs compared with national expectations for pupils of the same ability. The data consistently shows that Trinity pupils achieve, on average and across every subject, at least one grade higher at GCSE than would be expected from their cognitive abilities. Some of them achieve very much higher than this.

Other fears have also proved groundless. Far from being socially inadequate, the graduates of Trinity School are often regarded as exceptional by local sixth form colleges and employers. One college stated, 'We feared that the group that was about to transfer to us from Trinity would prove to be narrow and socially inadequate. In the event, it was the exact opposite. The young people were a great asset to their classes. They knew how to debate but treated others with courtesy and consideration. They enriched the life of the college by their involvement in and leadership of several societies.' These remarks were made in about 1990, but similar stories are being told down to the present day.

Crisis, provision and growth
Once the Trinity family was settled back in Stalybridge, numbers grew steadily and the school prospered in many ways. In 1988, Ross Evans joined Sylvia Baker in the leadership of the school, a partnership that was to continue for many years. However, financially, things did not get any easier. The school was still financed on a contribution basis. Families were asked to give what they could afford. In 1990, a major financial crisis

meant that radical action had to be taken and it was decided to move to a fee-paying situation. However, the fees were kept as low as possible and were charged on a family basis, rather than per child.

Now that Trinity School was established, and regularly coming top of the league tables, many more families began to express an interest in sending their children. It is carefully explained to all those who approach the school that Trinity is not an average private school, but is committed to a radical view of education that tries to put the Lord Jesus in the centre. Over the years many people, both children and adults, have become Christians through their association with Trinity. The school community, imperfect though it inevitably is, makes Christianity visible.

After the crisis of 1990 had passed, the numbers of pupils grew again until the building began to feel very overcrowded. In 1995, a further building was obtained to house the younger part of the school and this permitted further growth. As the 26th year of the school's life approaches its conclusion, there are about 140 children on the current roll and more than 450 past pupils, the oldest of whom are now in their mid thirties. The tiny venture that began with seven children has now affected about 600.

Trinity School must close? People may have thought so in 1979, but God had other plans. This school, pioneering Christian schooling in constantly difficult circumstances, is a testimony to the mercy of God and to the way in which His power works best in our weakness.

Letters

One of those who had opposed Trinity School throughout the eighties was a Christian science teacher, Paul Taylor, who taught at a local comprehensive school. In 1990,

Paul moved away from the area. In September, 2003, the school received a gracious letter from him.

'I thought it was time I wrote to you because in the past we used to differ over the subject of Christian education. I have now come to the view that my previous opposition to independent Christian education was wrong. I hope it is OK that it has taken me 20 years to work out that I was wrong.

I now see a society ever more out of touch with God. I see an education system ever more geared to training young people away from Christian values. I now believe that a school such as yours, open to the public but working with Christian staff in a Christian ethos is a valuable and powerful witness to the nation.

I am sorry that my previous views caused difficulties for Trinity School in days gone by.

Paul Taylor'

What do former pupils say?

'My two years at Trinity were the happiest of my child hood.'

'My education at Trinity made me an excellent listener to others and to think of others before myself. We were taught by example, not just the text book.'

'Trinity provided a really good foundation of truth about moral issues and God's perspective on things. I have come away with only positive memories. I praise God for what he started in me then and that He is still very much at work in my life.'

'My Christian faith has been strengthened by the ability to "think Christianly" and Trinity equipped me to approach life this way.'

'I am grateful to Trinity for a basis and a grounding in God's word, his values and high expectations, without which I am sure I would not be where I am today. I'm now blessed enough to be teaching in a Christian school myself, trying with God's grace to give to children what you gave to me, hope, ambition and a stable knowledge that God loves his children.'

O, people, the Lord has already told you what is good, and this is what he requires: to do what is right, to love mercy, and to walk humbly with your God (Micah 6:8).

> *'I would advise no-one to send his child where the holy Scriptures are not supreme. Every institution which does not unceasingly pursue the study of God's word becomes corrupt.'*
> Martin Luther

3

A close community

Immanuel School, Romford

A very unusual school

One of the most unusual of the new Christian schools is to be found in Romford, Essex. Founded in 1980, in its early days this school would have appeared to fulfil all the dire predictions that were coming from the lips of the opponents of Christian schools, yet it is one of the most successful of the schools when measured by the spiritual walk and commitment of its former pupils. Whereas other Christian schools were started after years, or at least months, of careful planning, the school at Romford opened within a few weeks of their first meeting. Other schools may have spent months trying to get a permanent building established; in Romford, this situation went on for years! Yet the end result of what might have seemed to be years of chaos and confusion is an army of young adults strongly committed to following God, heading up churches, leading in worship, teaching in the school they once attended and keen to place their own children into Christian schools.

Where did it all begin, and why has it been so successful?

Born out of community

In the late seventies and early eighties, several families, all members of the same church, were living as a close community. They shared all their belongings and lived close to one another. The mums looked after each other's babies and they ran an informal playgroup in their homes to give each other a free morning. To open a school just seemed like a natural progression of this way of life. Their church considered children to be very important. The aim of the whole church was to pass on their faith and values to the children and to help the parents to be involved in their children's education.

As a result, nearly twenty-five years later, the school is still strongly based within the church. In fact, the church and school are so closely linked that they are not really separate entities and it is hard to speak of one without including the other. For the leaders of Immanuel Church, Immanuel School is an essential part of the way they fulfil their task of discipling the youngest members of the church family. The fact that the church operates as a close community, seeing their church life as a natural part of their overall lifestyle, provides a secure environment. The strong bonds that exist between the members of the church have helped to give them the confidence to step out in ways of which other Christians might be fearful. From the beginning, both the church and the school have been willing to be risk-takers and to follow the prompting of the Holy Spirit, even when it leads to radical action.

The young people of the church and school are encouraged early on into leadership positions. It is not unusual to see former pupils helping to teach in the school within two years of taking their GCSEs. By their early 20s, they are encouraged to take up positions of responsibility within the church.

A radical approach to sixth form studies

Recently, the church has launched a course called 'Eagles Nest' aimed at young people aged between 16 and 35. This means that students do not have to transfer to other schools or colleges at the age of 16, but can combine 'A' level education with further theological and spiritual training. The theological part of the course is provided by St. John's College, Nottingham, with whom the church has entered into partnership. It leads to a Certificate in Christian Studies, which can provide a foundation for going on to study for a Diploma and then a Degree in theology. For those taking the 'A' level option, in year one, students follow the Eagles' Nest course, working for the Certificate in Christian Studies. In years two and three, they continue to spend 9–11 a.m. in prayer, worship and Biblical teaching with the other Eagles' Nest students, but work for three or four 'A' levels during the rest of the day.

The unity and close working relationship of the church and school give Immanuel great strength and are part of the reason for their success.

What do former pupils say?

'I spent quite a lot of my time in the school rebelling and wanting to go to a state school. But now I look back on my time in the school as a major part of my testimony. I see that God really had his hand on my life and that He was drawing me and teaching me a lot. With the foundations that were put in me at that stage I have been able to live as a strong Christian in whatever situation I have found myself. There is no question as to where my kids are going. I would definitely send them to a Christian school.'

'I firmly believe in what the school is doing. I appreciated then, and appreciate it even more now, being taught the truth and being educated with a "Jesus" focus and a family feel. I am very grateful to the school for encouraging my walk with God and teaching me with care, looking out for my spiritual and emotional development as well as the intellectual.

Real Christian education is very close to my heart and it is what I desire for my children.'

'I thank God for putting me in the fortunate place of being able to go to Immanuel and be taught by wonderful godly teachers. I owe a lot to the school.'

'I would say that the school provided a large part of the foundation of my faith. It was very obvious that we were all liked and valued by the teachers. All our lessons were very relational. The atmosphere in the school was much more conducive to learning and developing a relationship with God than that of the college I later attended.'

The vision statement of Immanuel School:
'Children who know God and are equipped to live in the light of that knowledge.'

Whatever you do or say, let it be as a representative of the Lord Jesus (Col. 3:17).

4

David and Goliath?

Christian Fellowship School, Liverpool

Dawning realisation of a need

The story in Liverpool began in about 1970 when a young teacher, Phil Williamson, taught for two years at a large comprehensive. Phil then had the opportunity to spend eight months abroad. When he returned to teaching in Liverpool, he noticed that in just that short time there had been a decline in standards and behaviour amongst the pupils. Having taught for a further two years, he returned to Africa for a year. Coming back to the UK, he was pleased to be able to get a teaching position in what was considered to be a model comprehensive school. However, a further decline in standards was very noticeable to him.

This pattern of working abroad and then coming back to the UK to teach was to be repeated several times. Each return home brought a further sense of shock at the declining standards. What exactly was it that Phil was reacting to? He found that the general atmosphere in the British schools was unruly. It was as though the children ruled in the corridors and thoroughfares. There was a noticeable decline in respect for teachers. Good teachers were not able to teach well because some individual pupils would be so disruptive. Phil began to think, 'What are we sending our children to? There must be something better than this.'

At the same time, the content of some of the teaching gave Phil great cause for concern. In science, his own subject, evolution was taught unquestioningly, providing an atheist framework for what was studied. In religious studies, the approach to teaching the Bible was to assume that it was not necessarily true. Phil realised that far from being a neutral approach, this was subversively introducing a particular view of the Bible.

Towards the beginning

Phil decided to approach the two churches that he had connections with, Devonshire Road and Litherland Christian Fellowships. He explained his concerns, his conviction that they must provide something better in the way of schooling for the children of the church. The two fellowships gave Phil their backing and committed themselves to help fund the work and find premises and staff. In faith, some parents decided to commit their children to the as yet non-existent school and two church members, Barbara Lord and Carol Jerman, were approached about becoming its first teachers. So it was that in the autumn of 1980, Christian Fellowship School was on its way to becoming a reality.

The next challenge was to find suitable premises for the school. After they had searched for some time with no success, the Devonshire Road Fellowship offered them the use of some basement rooms in one of the houses that the church owned. A lot of work would be necessary to bring the accommodation up to the necessary standard. The future head, teachers and parents of the school, helped by other friends from the fellowships, worked together cleaning, painting and wallpapering. The garden at the back of the house was flagged to create a playground.

At the same time, Phil, Barbara and Carol began to rethink what they knew of education. It was a process that was to take many years and indeed is still ongoing. In those early days, certain principles became clear.

- Christian education involves character building.
- Christian education requires a Christian curriculum.
- Protection from destructive influences and pressures at an early age results in strength to withstand these when the child is older.
- They had to act out of conviction, not preference or convenience.
- Consistent exposure to what is right develops the ability to recognise what is right.

The adventure begins

At last the hard work of making preparations was over. In February 1981, Christian Fellowship School opened with 30 children aged between four and fourteen, a headmaster, two teachers and a small group of volunteers. With no state funding it was necessary to charge fees but these were kept as low as possible as most of the families were anything but wealthy. Coming to the school was not a soft option for the pupils. They were protected from harmful influences but as far as accountability for their own conduct and work was concerned, there was no hiding place, no crowd to disappear amongst. The staff did their best to be supportive and encouraging, believing that the children were being given the opportunity to face the right kind of difficulties while being shielded from the wrong kind.

When the school opened in February 1981, they were still waiting for planning permission for change of use. The planning application had to go to a council vote and shortly after the school opened, they received a visit from a large group of city councillors. They saw for themselves how the basement area had been transformed, how light it was and how well the children's needs were being catered for. Permission for change of use was belatedly granted by a majority of just one vote and a major hurdle removed. The school could easily have died in its first term!

A new home

From the beginning, the school looked for larger premises, and eventually the building housing Liverpool Bible College came up for sale. This was 1, Princes Road, less than half a mile away from their existing site. It would give the school space to develop and grow and seemed to be ideal for the next stage of the school's life. The Devonshire Road Fellowship agreed to buy the property, primarily for the use of the school. During that summer, while negotiations for the building were taking place, the whole area was dramatically disrupted by the Toxteth riots. The building just across the road was totally destroyed by fire and other buildings blazed in the near vicinity, but 1, Princes Road was unscathed.

In September 1982, the school moved into 1, Princes Road with over forty children and two more teachers. A time of quick growth and rapid change followed as, over the next four years, the staff team expanded rapidly and the four classes blossomed into nine. As the school grew larger, it developed into Lower, Middle and Upper Schools, serving the age groups 4-8, 8-13 and 13-16. These particular groupings were chosen because they represent the stages of development recognised in the Hebrew tradition. As the numbers grew, so too did the range of churches represented by the school families.

The growing vision

The teachers of Christian Fellowship School had received their initial training in Christian education under the A.C.E. system. This had provided them with some important foundational ideas. To train up a child according to Christian, Biblical principles involved encouragement and correction, rewards and sanctions. The emphasis though was always on encouragement. It was important to give the child responsibilities in work and conduct, tailored to his or her level of ability. Children should become active learners, well motivated and equipped with study skills so that they could read to learn. They were to be equipped with the skills and character qualities that would enable them to become leaders. They should be protected from destructive influences early so that they could be strong later. The curriculum should be biblical. A child should never be humiliated. Corporal punishment, properly, kindly and lovingly administered, played a part in God's order.

As the teachers worked with these principles, it occurred to them that a main reason for setting up the school was to protect the child's conscience. They thought of the pressures on most school children from Christian homes to go against what their parents had taught them, and how hard it was for them to resist these influences, especially in their early teens, when peer pressure was so great. Most would compromise what they had been taught at home, although this would give them an uneasy feeling. For many, the way to get rid of the bad feeling would be to lose the faith that their parents had tried to impart to them. These thoughts seemed to be well summed up by 1 Timothy 1:19, which says, '*Cling tightly to your faith in Christ, and always keep your conscience clear. For some people have deliberately violated their consciences; as a result, their faith has been shipwrecked.*' It began not to seem surprising that it is so hard to secure each new generation for Christ.

For various reasons, the school decided only to use the complete A.C.E. system for about the first eighteen months, although they remained grateful for the good principles that it had introduced them to. They began to look at other curriculum models and to seek the Lord for the right way forward. They realised that in developing a Christ-centred curriculum there was a need to pray for guidance and understanding. Teachers could pray for help in choosing the right approach for a particular class. They needed to learn to listen to God and to study the Bible. They also began to see how important it was to model their own methods on the approach that Jesus himself took to teaching. For example, Jesus asked questions, told stories and took many illustrations from everyday life.

By 1987, the school had nearly 200 pupils and was achieving very good results. However, there was also an urgent need for bigger and more suitable premises. Their building, which had seemed so roomy at first, was now completely full. A search began which was to take ten years. Buildings that had formerly housed schools quite often came onto the market in Liverpool. Despite much prayer and many approaches, the school was never permitted to buy any of these properties. It was discouraging that the process of finding somewhere new should take such a long time, but when the answer to prayer eventually came it was well worth waiting for.

Answered Prayer
In 1996 came the answer to prayer they had been looking for. A large school building in Overbury Street came on to the market. A former Roman Catholic school, and still owned by the Catholic archdiocese, the trust deed of this building would not permit the land to be used for property development. The school negotiated a price, £150,000, which turned out to be the same amount as their current building was worth, and the

archdiocese allowed them to arrange to move in immediately without waiting for their old building to be sold. Phil and a governor returned to the new building, which they had previously inspected closely, to have another look round. To their horror they found that it had been completely vandalised, even though a security firm had been employed to protect it. When they had looked at it originally, it had been in very good condition. Now the copper piping had been ripped out, the main water tank had burst and water was streaming through the whole structure. There were gaping holes in some of the floors. Everywhere was filthy and there were many broken windows. Outside the grass was waist high.

As soon as the archdiocese became aware of what had happened, they undertook to put the situation right. The school was given £80,000 to effect repairs. This meant that they could redevelop the building to suit their own requirements. They knocked walls down to create extra classrooms and had the building professionally rewired and replumbed. The rest of the work the school did themselves to keep costs down. For months staff, governors, parents, former pupils and friends of the school worked there night after night and on Saturdays. They cleaned, decorated, did minor repairs and sorted out the grounds.

In March, 1997, Christian Fellowship School was able to move into its impressive new home. The sense of space was wonderful – a whole building full of rooms big enough to take 25 pupils, science labs, art rooms, a large library, an expressive arts room, a computer room, a technology room, a staff room, a good-sized hall and stage, the list seemed endless! In the end it took them over a year to sell their old building and in all that time the archdiocese did not require any payments from them. When the former building was finally sold and they were able to settle their debts, everything balanced to the penny. At the end of the process, they did not owe one penny to anybody.

A difficult calling

By late 1997, it seemed as though many of the major battles were over. The school had a wonderful building with plenty of space to expand into. They had now been well-established for many years and were developing a very good reputation. However, in 1998 something happened which was to project the school into the limelight and which proved to be the start of a long and difficult battle. In March, 1998, The House of Commons voted in favour of an amendment to outlaw corporal punishment in independent schools, as part of the School Standards and Framework bill. Many people throughout the country felt that this was an infringement of parental rights and religious liberty.

At Christian Fellowship School, a special meeting was called of parents, staff and governors to discuss the implications of what was happening. The main movers behind the changes appeared to be the small committee of EPOCH, whose ultimate aim is for it to become illegal for parents to smack their own children. These individuals had worked very hard for many years to achieve change. The school felt that it was important to resist this change in the law as much as they could because they felt that at a later date not only the school would be affected but homes as well. Something had to be done and first they would voice their objections. Other Christian schools were contacted and about fifty of them agreed that action needed to be taken. Phil would take the matter forward on behalf of all these schools.

In the spotlight

Very quickly, the media descended on the school. Reporters from newspapers, radio and TV became commonplace. Various parents, members of staff and pupils had to be ready at a moment's notice to add their voices to the debate but of course it was to be Phil himself who was to be the main spokesman.

The law came into effect in the summer of 1999. The staff, governors and parents of Christian Fellowship School were as concerned as anyone that children should not be abused and agreed that the hitting of children could be abusive, if wrongly or excessively carried out. They believed, however, that a limited use of corporal punishment, mainly in the form of a smack to young children, was anything but abusive. Properly used, it assisted the child's training and development and should only be used to that end, never out of adult frustration.

A wider issue

A wider issue was also at stake. It seemed that the Government was acting to tell Christians how to interpret their faith, since the school was basing its position on the teaching of Bible passages. This was a major point of principle, and if allowed to pass unchallenged could form a precedent for the practice of Christianity to be restricted in other ways as well.

The school began the process of taking the matter to the European Court at Strasbourg. This was a long and complicated task and involved Phil in a great deal of work. Late in 2000, the European Court ruled that the school had no case to bring. The British Government had not, in fact, banned corporal punishment in independent schools if the parents had specifically delegated their authority to the school, in writing, to smack on their behalf if it were deemed necessary.

To the High Court

The next step was to take the DfEE to the British High Court for infringement of religious freedom and parental rights. Other Christian schools contributed to the considerable costs, and again Phil gave much of his valuable time. At the end of

November 2001, the case went to court and the judge ruled in favour of the DfEE.

The decision to mount an appeal against this decision was not taken lightly. Well aware of what the cost would be in terms of time and money, Phil and the others at the school still felt the weight of the original reasons for taking up the battle. It was too important to give up now.

A dangerous precedent

The Court of Appeal heard the case in May 2003. After one day's hearing, they took six months to decide that they needed another hearing. Eventually a weighty document was produced, turning down the appeal on the grounds that the issue of discipline was not central to religious belief. For the first time, a British court had taken it upon itself to decide what was central to religious belief and what was not. Effectively, a secular court had decided how the Christian faith should be practised. Phil and his legal advisors found this to be such a dangerous precedent that the case is being taken to the House of Lords.

David against Goliath?

Christian Fellowship School, along with the other participating Christian schools, has been criticised for its decision to involve itself with the issue of corporal punishment. However, Phil and those supporting him feel that they have very good reason for the stand that they have taken. They are praying that the issue of child abuse will not be confused with godly discipline. They want the rising tide of lawlessness in our state schools and its mirrored effects in society of escalating youth crime to be recognised and acknowledged. They also believe that there are wider issues at stake than just that of corporal punishment. The root issue is the right of parents to exercise Christian choices for their children. They are very concerned that the State has imposed a humanistic philosophy not just over its own state schools but over the independent schools which until recently were so free to follow the wishes of the parents.

David up against Goliath – that's how it looks as Phil prepares to take this case to the House of Lords. A small Christian school has been drawn into the forefront of the battle between historic Christianity and the increasing influence of secular humanism and other world views. It remains to be seen what the outcome will be.

What do some former pupils say?

'I would like to thank the staff for their love, personal time and school input which enabled me to not only discover my educational potential but to develop as a person and Christian in a loving secure environment.'

'The school enabled me to solidify my Christian beliefs. This gave better preparation for the "real world" than I would have had with standard comprehensive education.'

'I'm very thankful to have been at a school that reinforced the Christian principles of home.

I value the foundation of these principles far more than any academic achievement – which I also got anyway!'

Teach your children to choose the right path and when they are older they will remain upon it (Prov. 22:6).

> *'I am much afraid that schools will prove to be the great gates of hell unless they diligently labour in explaining the Holy Scriptures, engraving them on the hearts of youth.'*
> Martin Luther

5

A Family School

Covenant Christian School, Stockport

A group meets

In the 1970s, a number of Christian teachers from the Stockport area decided to meet together to look at what the Bible has to say about education. Their studies led them to the conclusion that parents have the main responsibility for the education of their children and that the home is central to a child's development. They came to believe that the role of the school is to back up and support the parents as they try to fulfil this responsibility and that as far as possible the Christian school should function like an extension of a Christian home.

The group then decided to study what the aims of a Christian school should be and compared their findings with a government green paper that had just been issued. They contacted local schools and asked them what their aims were, only to find that at that time schools usually didn't have any! By this time, several of the group had children of their own. They began to realise that the local schools could not provide the type of education that the Bible urges parents to pursue.

The school begins

One couple, Roger and Ruth Slack, owned a fairly large house and it was here that the school began, with just three children, in March 1981. Planning permission for ten children had been granted, but numbers of potential pupils quickly grew beyond this. Roger and Ruth began to look for a bigger house. They saw a particular property in their area of Stockport that looked exceptionally suitable, but it was not for sale. They did not think for one minute that it would ever become available or that if it did, they would be able to obtain it.

A new home

In 1985, Ruth began to suspect that one of the estate agents was not bothering to inform them when suitable properties came on to the market. She phoned to complain. The estate agent was very apologetic and said, 'As it happens, a property has just become available….' It was THE house! From then on, it was obvious that God's hand was on the transaction. It was as though they had a green light all the way. Roger and Ruth sold their existing house, the new one was obtained at a very reasonable price and planning permission to use the property as a school was readily granted. The plan was to use some of the rooms in the house as classrooms, to convert the cellar to provide both a science lab and a craft room and to refurbish a coach house on the property to provide three more classrooms. The school's numbers would then be able to rise to more than 40. In November 1985, the school moved in.

A good report

Almost 20 years later, in February 2004, Covenant School became one of the first of the new Christian schools to be inspected under new, more rigorous arrangements. The published report prepared by the Office for Standards in

Education (Ofsted) commended the school for its well thought out religious and philosophical basis. The inspectors considered that the education that the pupils were receiving would prepare them well for further and higher education and for life in the outside world. They especially commented on the good relationships and excellent behaviour that they observed in the school.

A family school

As the Ofsted inspectors were able to discern, Covenant School gives a high priority to the family. Parents are expected to participate fully in the life of the school and they do so by offering their services for teaching, maintenance, administration and anything else that needs to be done!

In the early 1990s, Roger and Ruth became aware of the increasing numbers of Christians in the UK who were choosing to educate their children at home. They realised that some of these parents were feeling isolated and needed support. They decided to start a network, which initially linked 12 families. By 2004 this had grown to 500 families catering for about 800-900 children. Roger and Ruth provide a regular newsletter, a resource guide, a contacts list, a tape library, local workshops and a national conference every two years. Local home-schoolers join Covenant School for swimming sessions, borrow their science lab and sit their public exams at the school.

Covenant Christian School and their link with the Home School movement help to illustrate that Christian education in the UK operates on a spectrum running from those who educate at home, through small family-type schools, to larger schools organised on a more traditional basis. All of these approaches are successful; what makes the difference is the centrality of Jesus and the living word of God.

Former pupils say:

'I think that I benefited greatly from going to the school. Some say that the pupils would be overprotected and know nothing about the world and that Christians should be alongside non-Christians to witness. I think that young Christians do need protecting and that a young, new Christian at a "normal" school would be more likely to be affected than to affect anyone else. Overall, school was a brilliant experience.'

'The more I progress with life, the more I miss school and the environment it created for me. The greatest thing that was gained from school was undoubtedly the Christian environment and atmosphere which I was taught in and which I really miss now.'

'A Covenant education is a unique experience and one which it is a privilege to receive. The quality of education on an academic level is excellent and the care and personal attention which teachers are able to offer is brilliant, The spiritual grounding which is offered as part of your everyday experience is possibly the most valuable schooling you can ever receive. Overall I look back on my experiences at Covenant with great fondness, something I might have found unlikely at the time!'

You must commit yourself wholeheartedly to these commands I am giving you today. Repeat them again and again to your children. Talk about them when you are at home and when you are away on a journey, when you are lying down and when you are getting up again (Deut. 6:6-7).

6

The King's School, Basingstoke

The King's School was founded in September 1981 and is part of the ministry of Basingstoke Community Churches, a group of six local churches with over a thousand members. All 170 pupils belong to families attending one or other of the churches.

In February 2004, The King's School also became one of the first of the new Christian schools to be inspected by Ofsted (the Office for Standards in Education) under the new, more rigorous, inspection arrangements. The inspectors reported that they found it to be a very good school, producing happy and well-prepared pupils. They considered some lessons to be of outstanding quality and that the school's Christian philosophy was underpinning much of its success.

A newly appointed teacher, Ann Raine, tells of the impact that the school has had on her.

'I have been in education for 30 years, teaching across the spectrum from nursery to adult, including helping those with special needs. Throughout this time I was a Christian and I used to ask God to help me to be an excellent teacher. I felt that He answered this prayer and considered my teaching to be of a good standard.

In September 2003, I arrived at the King's School in Basingstoke, where I had offered, as a volunteer, to teach GCSE child development and to help with learning support. I was amazed at the philosophy of education that I saw underlying everything there. The atmosphere hit me as soon as I arrived as I sensed the Holy Spirit's presence throughout the school. I saw teachers praying for pupils and pupils praying for each other.

I spent most of the following year crying, especially during assemblies. I was so moved by what I saw and felt that God was touching my life in a new way.

I now understand that Christian education is something radically different from the approach that I was used to, that it involves discipling as well as teaching knowledge. I now see that education belongs to God and that He should be involved in every part of it. From now on I will ask Him to guide me in every detail. For the first time, I see my responsibility to pray for all the children in my care and to ask God to reveal to me the best way to teach them.'

The Lord will be your sure foundation, providing a rich store of salvation, wisdom and knowledge. The fear of the Lord is the key to this treasure (Isa. 33:6).

> *'True religion affords government its surest support. The future of this nation depends on the Christian training of the youth. It is impossible to govern without the Bible.'*
> George Washington

7

The King's School, Southampton

The King's School, Southampton opened its doors in September 1982. On that first day there were 35 pupils. Members of Southampton Community Church believed that God had told them to start the school. Geoff Wright, the school's first head teacher recalls, 'The whole venture was an example of parent/teacher co-operation. It gave real meaning to the phrase "in loco parentis". Parents gave money, time, skills, encouragement and their experience to the school, but they also handed over their children to us during school hours on the unspoken understanding that we would do for their children what they would have done, had they the time and the ability. Their total support was not only vital, but also very touching.'

From its modest beginning in 1982, by the time of its 21st anniversary, the school had grown to become three schools, separate primary and secondary schools in Southampton and a primary school in Winchester.

Former pupils say:
'Being a Christian in the school was so much easier. I

loved the Friday assemblies when we pupils would lead the worship and sometimes bring the word. It was really encouraging and challenging. The sport was great fun; even though we didn't have much, it was still so much fun!'

'I loved my time at the school and have only fond memories. I loved the safe environment, the opportunity to form close and lasting friendships, the freedom to be creative and to grow in my faith. The school gave me a firm moral grounding and a perspective on life that has been challenged but has lasted.

Although the school was small and different, I grew to enjoy the fact that I was part of something unique and special. In this way, the school prepared me for my Christian walk – that as a Christian I am set apart from the world, but still secure in the Lord.

The older I get, the fewer criticisms I have of the school. I don't think I was deprived of anything by being there. In fact, I feel privileged to have gone. If I was "sheltered" by being at the school, then I was sheltered from all the things that a child should be protected from. Although my faith has been challenged and tested in the years since leaving the school, I have never lost the perspective and grounding in truth that a Christian education provided.'

Fear of the LORD is the beginning of knowledge. Only fools despise wisdom and discipline (Prov. 1:7).

8

The Swans

The King's School, Witney, Oxfordshire

One Sunday in March 1983, something special happened at a meeting of the Oxfordshire Community Churches. The two speakers that day were dealing with the subject of Christian education and at one point they asked all those children who were under nine years of age to stand on their chairs. As they did so, the eyes of the church were opened to see the great importance of those children in God's eyes, how very high they were on his agenda.

Months of planning and praying followed that meeting, as the five churches met together to seek God. A strong sense of unity and faith developed, together with an increasing excitement. It seemed that God was indeed calling them to establish a Christian school and they believed that they should try to achieve this by September 1984.

David Freeman and Geoff Norridge, who both had teaching experience, were asked to visit other Christian schools to see what they could learn from them. However, at this point David, who was leading a small church, had no idea that he was destined to become the principal of the new school that was being planned!

Not even a drawing pin!

After much prayer, it became clear that David was the one God had appointed to establish the Christian school. At first he felt overwhelmed at the enormity of the task that faced him. He would be starting a school from scratch; they had absolutely nothing, not even a drawing pin! Where would they start? To be a Head at all was a big enough task, but to head up a school for God's children seemed totally beyond any of them – as indeed it was. But they were all to learn that God is able to use those who feel inadequate, because they are forced to rely exclusively on his great wisdom, strength and power.

After David had been appointed Principal of the, as yet, nonexistent school, the next step was to find some teachers. Within weeks, Julia Morgan and Keith Elmitt had joined the staff and these were to prove key appointments. Twenty years later, they are still hard at it, serving the school as Heads of Lower and Upper School respectively.

In April 1984, the new staff held their first meeting. It was unlike any other staff meeting that they had ever experienced! They prayed, broke bread together, and then set about deciding on the curriculum and what they would need to purchase. As they sat round a table delving into catalogues, they were both excited and overwhelmed at the huge task that lay before them.

Throughout the summer months that followed, family after family were interviewed and eventually 77 children aged between five and thirteen had been enrolled for the new school. They represented all the different congregations in the Oxfordshire Community Churches. As the time drew near to open the school, several people took David on one side to express their concern about the risk to their children's future. 'How do you know that you are not jeopardising their future?' they asked. 'How do you know it will work?' The honest answer had to be that David and his team didn't know! Time would tell. Jesus said that you will know the tree by its fruit and those who questioned the wisdom of what the Witney team were doing were asked to come back years later to assess the fruit. That time has now arrived and the results can be seen in the excellent academic results and exemplary characters of former students.

Nowhere to go?

A policy decision made at the beginning was to use, temporarily at least, the American system known as Accelerated Christian Education. It was to prove a wise decision in the early days when it unexpectedly became necessary to be able to teach 'on the move.' As September 1984 approached, the staff, pupils, curriculum and uniform were all in place. However, there was one rather big problem – no building! God had been speaking to the team through a verse from Proverbs 24. '*By wisdom a house is built, by understanding it is established and by knowledge the rooms are filled with rare and beautiful treasures.*' These were wonderful thoughts, but right now God did not seem to be very practical – they had nowhere to go! One building was available, Merryfield House, but although it was a beautiful building it was considered impractical and undesirable as a school. With two weeks to go to the opening of the school, they began moving into Merryfield House with many misgivings but no other choice.

There were certainly some problems with the use of Merryfield House. The Infants had to be upstairs with no running water or art area. The rest of the school – 50 of them in three classes with three teachers – had to fit into one large lounge and an adjoining dining room. Over the next few months, the teachers became expert at keeping their voices pitched only for their own pupils, asking one another if it was all right to speak for any length of time. In this way, real family links were formed between them. They were forced to relate over everything.

Right at the start, the new school received great encouragement when all the children, neat and tidy in their new uniforms, walked into a celebration meeting at which the churches had gathered together. The churches were challenged and inspired by seeing them and a clear prophetic word was given. The school was to be like a beehive; each of the children were to be 'busy bees', working hard, and the school would produce quality honey which would be exported all over the world. Those who know the Witney School well can testify to how true this has proved to be in practice.

The first year

On the morning the school opened, David felt very nervous. Would they be able to get the school off to a good start? Were they jeopardising their children's future and risking their future careers? Yet they had to obey the leading God had so clearly given them. Soon cars began to arrive at the Merryfield House car park and pupils, spick and span in their new uniforms, streamed into school to find their places. They began the King's School with the first of many assemblies where they gave thanks to God. 'Lord, we stand on your word. We declare your victory. Lift up a standard as the light of the world!' This became their theme song throughout the first year.

That first year whizzed by. There was much to be learned – both by pupils and by staff! An army of parents and friends came in regularly to help with monitoring, teaching, hearing readers and cleaning. Although the work was exhausting for all the staff, there was a real thrill in knowing that they were fulfilling the Lord's will.

Battle

As is so often the case, while God was blessing and establishing the school, the enemy was hard at work, stirring up trouble. In the early months, the local paper carried adverse publicity, under such headlines as, '**Noisy contentious Christian school**.' Some of the neighbours had complained, angry that a school had opened right next to them. The school did their best to be polite and careful and other local people took a different view, describing the pupils as the best and most polite children they had ever met. Nevertheless, the problem remained.

While everyone was on holiday in August, recovering from the hard work of that first year, the message was received that a Stop Order had been placed on the school by the local council authorities. This meant that the school had to stop running immediately! With only two weeks to go to the beginning of term, there was no option but to vacate the premises. What were they to do? This was battle, and everyone began to pray for God to provide for the school's immediate needs, while an appeal was organised, a process that would take months.

Big Bend!

At the start of the year, the school had received a prophecy that compared them to a family of swans swimming downstream. There would be turbulence, the prophecy said, the wind would ruffle their feathers and there would be several bends to negotiate, one of which would be like a U turn, prolonged and difficult. Eventually, they were promised, they would be led to a beautiful lake, a haven provided by God. Now was obviously the time of the turbulence and the big bend!

The night before the second school year should have begun, the Lord's provision came. Someone who had heard of their predicament phoned to offer them the use of the Bampton scout huts, which had originally been a primary school. How the school praised God for rescuing them at the last minute! Thus began a hard period of slog and survival as the school had to be packed into cardboard boxes every weekend so that the scouts could use the rooms. Every Sunday evening, faithful leaders and parents turned out to help set up school again, ready for Monday morning. Both teachers and pupils realised that God was teaching them that to follow Jesus was not always easy.

Conditions became more and more demanding as different organisations wished to use the rooms on other evenings, and the school had to be packed up more and more often. The crunch came in late October when they were told that they would have to leave within a week as the huts were needed. On receiving this news, the school gathered for a special assembly where the students both praised God and prayed as never before. It stunned all of them that within an hour of this assembly a messenger arrived with a note, saying that they would be able to stay until Christmas.

This gave a welcome breathing space, but what then? The school had to accept that, for a time at least, they had become a pilgrim people.

At the end of October, the Appeal was heard. The barrister who was acting for the school felt that they had a very strong case. Some of the senior students were present, watching and praying, and everyone felt that there was hope of a positive outcome. However, a decision was not likely to be given for several months. What was the school to do in the meantime?

To the zoo!

After Christmas, urgent phone calls tracked down some meeting rooms – at Cotswold Wild Life Park at Burford! There was no other alternative and so, briefly as it turned out, they became the school at the zoo! One class was in the room over the reptile house, with accompanying smells and echoing shrieks from the nearby monkey and parrot cages. Of course, the children thought it was wonderful. At the first assembly, as they sniffed the strange-smelling air, David told the children that wherever God placed them, they would take the fragrance of Jesus Christ. As the assembly finished, a message arrived. They had won the Appeal; the answer had come in six weeks instead of several months and they could return to Merryfield House immediately! The big bend of the prophecy had been negotiated and with great joy on the part of the staff, with reluctance on the part of the children, they went back to Merryfield House which seemed to welcome them with the peace of God.

Growth and development

During the whole of the difficult time, the parents had loyally supported the school without one word of complaint. Not one child had been withdrawn. In fact, the problem had been in the other direction. Despite being nomads, the school had attracted new pupils. Numbers had reached 90, too many to fit back into Merryfield House! The Infant Department therefore had to use a hired hall in a nearby village, an arrangement that was not ideal.

The church leadership began to look for a large property within a seven-mile radius. They found absolutely nothing. With their backs to the wall, they felt that God was saying, 'I want you to build a new building.' At the beginning, the church and school community would not have had faith for this, but by now they had seen how God had provided for them through all the difficulties of the past year. They were also seeing how being at the school was blessing the children. They must move forward in faith now.

Buy a field!

There seemed to be nowhere in the immediate vicinity where the school could build but then contact was made with a local farmer who was willing to sell them a field, only a couple of hundred yards from Merryfield House! It was a local greenbelt area and much prayer went into the planning application. Permission was granted in January 1986. Now all that was needed was about £750,000!

That Easter, the next stage fell into place. It was necessary to do something for the following year. Merryfield House was bursting at the seams and the Infants, with Julia and Vera, needed to be brought back closer to home. It was then that the next piece of God's amazing jigsaw fell into place. The school was offered the use of some strong wooden huts which could be moved to the newly acquired field. They now had three large classrooms to house Infant, Junior and Middle School learning centres, plus an office. The Seniors would stay on at Merryfield House for the time being. In September 1986, the Lower School moved into the huts and in January 1987, work began on a purpose-built school. The school community remembered the prophecy about the final beautiful 'lake' that the 'swans' would have in which to nest and rear their young and they knew that this was it. A photo was taken of a rainbow over the field before excavation began. A year or so later another photo was taken of a rainbow in exactly the same place, only this time it arched over the beautiful new building. God had indeed fulfilled His promises.

Once they were established in the new premises, the staff wanted to write their own curriculum and gradually left the ACE system. This led eventually to the development of the curriculum, 'Foundations for Life', which has been widely used, both in England and abroad, fulfilling the original prophecy about the honey which would be exported all over the world.

After ten years of growth and blessing in the new premises, the school had once again outgrown the facilities. In September 1998, the seniors moved to their own premises in the centre of Witney and this allowed further growth to take place. In 2004 the numbers stand at 220 and yet again larger facilities are needed.

The fruit

The King's School are aware that they are a privileged community. As well as enjoying the support of a large network of churches, they are the only one of the new Christian Schools to benefit from a purpose-built building that they were able to design themselves. It soon became apparent that the Lord was calling them to a wider ministry, to look and work beyond their own absorbing situation. This wider work has come about on two fronts, both at home and abroad. In 1988, David was asked to visit Uganda to set up a school. This has led to further opportunities in Africa and also to the founding of a school in Kazakhstan. The children at the Witney School play a large part in supporting these ventures. Teams regularly visit Africa to help with projects. For example, in the summer of 2002, fourteen Year 11 students spent a fortnight in Zambia. They visited two schools and helped in several different ways, including erecting gates purchased with funds they had raised, painting friezes on classroom walls, teaching lessons and playing with the children. They worked very hard for the two weeks, without any complaints and with a servant spirit. They impressed many people, some of whom commented that now they could see that Christian education really works.

Yes, Minister!

At home in England, The King's School has been given a high profile by the Lord. In the late eighties 'important' people began to ask if they could visit. One of these was Angela Rumbold, who was then the deputy minister for education. As she toured the school, journalists flashed their cameras. One eventually asked her, 'What is your opinion of the school?'

'I give it top marks', she answered. She went on to say, 'There is a great sense of order and purpose about the school. The children I have talked to have been very articulate.... There is a good balance of curriculum. There is clearly more of a religious influence than would be found even in church-aided schools.... It is a refreshing change.'

The next day the same paper that a few years earlier had called the school 'noisy and contentious' carried the headline: **'EDUCATION MINISTER GIVES RELIGIOUS SCHOOL TOP MARKS.'**

God had vindicated the school in His own time and way!

In other ways, too, The King's School has become a leading part of the Christian schools movement in the UK. For many years, David has been part of the leadership of the Christian Schools' Trust. He has played a significant role in their conferences and in developing their teacher training programmes. This has led to many individuals visiting The King's School, either because they are interested in starting a Christian School, or because they already teach in one and want to learn from another situation. One of the highlights for the visitors is the opportunity to be prayed for by some of the children, who will often bring words of help and encouragement from the Lord. The school that was birthed in prophecy and sustained by words it itself received, is being used by God to bring this type of blessing to others.

The future

Only God knows what lies ahead for the King's School, Witney, but their desire is that He will lead them on 'from faith to faith'. They have been given much and they know that therefore much is required of them.

What do former pupils say?

'The further away I get from my school years the more I realise all the good life lessons and character attitudes that were invested in me. Since my parents were also Christians, all the principles I learnt at home were supported by those at school.'

'My favourite things about the King's School were the close relationships we were able to develop with the teachers and other pupils due to the school's small size and Christian atmosphere. In my Christian life, the King's School helped me to grow up a lot and become a much more mature Christian. This was especially due to teachers picking up character issues and giving a lot of opportunity for us to learn and grow as Christians. I don't think the King's School forced me in any way to be a Christian; instead it strengthened my faith and helped me think through issues and formulate my own opinions.'

'I am so pleased my parents were brave enough to send me to a Christian school. My personal view of Christian education is that it is invaluable. I cannot overstate how secure, grounded and precious I felt at the King's School, where teachers actively cared about who I was, not just what I knew. There was room for the realities of adolescence and in no way were we indoctrinated or forced into religion.'

> **The vision statement of The King's School:**
>
> *To produce young people who know God and are trained to serve and influence their generation by godly attitudes and actions.*

Don't be impressed with your own
wisdom. Instead, fear the Lord and turn
your back on evil (Prov. 3:7).

9

A dramatic story of provision

The River School, Worcester

September 1985 saw the culmination of yet another dramatic series of events in the opening of the River School in Worcester. The story began in the sixties and seventies when Duncan and Helen Crow were given a deep concern for the younger generation, which developed into a desire to see Christian schools established. During this time they shared their vision with their son Timothy who lived with his wife Joanna and young family in Worcester. Tim was teaching at the King's School in Worcester, a reputable independent school. Soon Tim and his wife Joanna were studying, discussing and praying, becoming ever more excited by the prospect of a special sort of education for their four young children. They realised that they wanted them to develop a godly, biblical worldview, to grow up in a spiritually sensitive atmosphere, and to be prepared to affect those around them with the power and truth of the Christian message.

Plans and dreams
The Crow parents and grandparents began to dream, think and plan for the establishment of a Christian school. At this

point it was little more than a family venture but Tim felt increasingly that God wanted others to be involved as well.

In 1981, Duncan Crow reached retirement age and was looking forward to becoming more involved in the Christian school venture. Suddenly, his health deteriorated rapidly and he died in August of that year. This unexpected blow put the vision of the school on hold for a while, but during that time a small prayer group of about ten people emerged who shared the vision and wanted to meet to pray about it. More parents and friends caught the vision and in 1983 Helen Crow came and settled in Worcester, keen to be involved in anything that God was doing on the Christian education front.

A step of faith

Meanwhile, Tim was seriously reconsidering his place on the staff at the King's School. He increasingly wanted the freedom to teach in a fully Christian way.

The prayer group was meeting once a week in his home and on one occasion they felt prompted to pray in a very specific way. They asked God, if he seriously wanted them to set up a school, to send them some money, however little, even one pound, before the next meeting. No-one was to mention this to anyone outside the meeting.

Joanna realised that the stakes were very high for the Crow family, especially in that Tim would perhaps need to resign from his job. The next morning she knelt down and prayed earnestly that God would not send anything, even one penny, unless he really wanted them to move out in faith. About half an hour later, there was a knock at the door. A friend was standing there, one who did not attend the prayer group and had no idea what had occurred the day before. She said, 'Look, here is £5.00. Start an account for this school you have talked about. It's time you started getting on with the project.' She quoted the epistle of

James, where it tells us not to waver. Joanna was speechless with amazement at the prompt answer to the prayers.

As a result of these events, Tim gave in his notice of resignation from his teaching position. He intended to leave at the end of the summer term.

Testing times

There were challenges to come. Amongst their friends at the local church in Worcester there was not wholehearted enthusiasm. The reaction was rather mixed and qualified. A number were clearly unconvinced by the vision of a Christian school, some were particularly concerned about the burden it might be upon the church if it accepted responsibility for a very costly venture, and some advised waiting because of the hesitation of others. This was an awkward experience for Tim and Joanna. They had taken a very costly decision, feeling that in all conscience before God this was what he required them to do, and they longed for the support of their church.

In the autumn, the prayer group was continuing to meet once a week. After a month or so, Tim sensed that God was asking them to stop meeting. This seemed absurd; it was as though they were giving up on all that Tim had left his job to pursue. However, they did not wish to be a divisive influence in their fellowship of Christians. It seemed that the Lord was asking them to surrender their project to him, sacrificing it in their hearts, rather like Abraham was asked to sacrifice Isaac. They would trust him to resurrect it in his good time. The final meeting of the prayer group was truly emotional. They knelt together in a circle and offered the vision of the school up to the Lord. They asked that the Lord would in time resurrect a multiplied number of prayer warriors. At that meeting there were seven of them. They asked the Lord for seventy-seven or more intercessors for the work.

For several months, nothing seemed to happen. It was not until March 1984 that eventually the local leaders in the church asked them to pick up the vision and pursue it again. They were not accepting responsibility for the venture, but they wanted the prayer group to reconvene and feel free to follow the guidance of the Lord. Once more they began to meet and the Lord began to speak.

The plan unfolds

During 1984, Helen Crow decided to visit some estate agents to see if there were any properties on the market that would be suitable for a small school. She discovered a converted church hall for sale, called Cleveland House. Joanna and one of the other intercessors, Norma Rogers, went to look over the property. Norma asked the Lord how she would know if this was his place for them. Immediately she felt the Lord give an answer, 'You will see red.' She wondered what this could possibly mean. The church hall had been sold to an industrial ventilation company who had thoroughly modernised the building. All the woodwork was painted a bright, pillar-box red. The skirting boards, the doorframes – even the telephones were red!

In the days that followed, others received similar confirmations and the group prayed with increased excitement. However, after a while their attention was drawn to another building – Oakfield House. This was owned by the local council and used as an educational resources centre. The grounds extended to eight and a half acres. This property was now coming on to the market and several people were led to go there and pray that God would procure and use the building.

A few months later, two things happened. The council invited tenders for Oakfield House and Cleveland House was withdrawn from the market. The group knew that God had clearly spoken to them about Cleveland House and they never forgot what he had said. However, it now looked as though they must pursue Oakfield House. The tenders were to be for £120,000 or more. After prayer, it was decided to offer £150,000, but the Council informed them that there had been an even higher bid.

The group invited a number of others to come and pray outside the building with them. They sang choruses of praise, marched around the building and asked the Lord to release the building to them. They prayed for the necessary finances, for the staff, for the pupils and for all the equipment. A lady from Malvern arrived. They had not met her before and she had never been there before but the Lord had given her a dream some months before in which she was outside a building just like this and witnessing the Lord providing for it. She literally wept as she realised that it was the building she had seen in her dream. The group knew more strongly than ever that the Lord was in this project; it was humbling to realise how much more he was teaching them about recognising his voice.

After a few more days, the group heard from the Council, inviting them to go and discuss their offer. The council officers explained that the development company that had made the higher bid had been refused planning permission and that their group was the next in line. The council was keen to explore their offer fully. Tim explained that they had so far only managed to collect £4,000, but that they had prayed and they believed that God would provide the full purchase money. The council was so keen to see them succeed that they extended the deadline for the payment of the deposit from two weeks to three months.

Raising the money

This meeting took place in October 1984 and they had until mid-January 1985 to find another £11,000. Tim did not believe that God wanted them to launch a major public appeal. If this was the Lord's venture, he could and would supply all that was needed. The group therefore once again gave themselves to prayer. Money began to come in. Over the last weekend, a rush of £4,000 arrived. One gift came in the form of a fat envelope put through Tim's letter-box containing £700 in notes. On the envelope was scrawled, 'For the School'. Three months later to the day, they had the needed £15,000.

The legal paperwork proceeded very slowly and it was not until June that everything was ready for completion. By this time, £90,000 had been received in gifts. The council officers were very impressed with the progress and realised that the school needed to be able to open in September. On September 4th, the situation was the same. No further substantial gifts had come in. The council officers said that the school could move in on three conditions: they would give them a short-term mortgage for the outstanding money, they had to sell off the lodge at the end of the drive which would raise £20,000 and one of the trustees needed to fulfil his offer to raise £30,000 to help bridge the gap.

On September 5th, they moved in with all their furniture and one week later, on September 12th 1985, The River School opened.

The school begins

The school opened with 35 pupils from 4 to 12 years of age, divided into two main classes. Many of the parents had taken steps of faith back in the summer and had notified their former schools that their children would not be returning in September, but would be starting at the new River School. The pupils came from a variety of backgrounds and churches.

The name 'The River School' was chosen from the book of Ezekiel where it talks about a river which flows from the throne of God and makes the trees on the banks fruitful in the land. They felt that the image spoke of all that they had prayed for with regard to the school – the flow of God's life, love, power and creativity, feeding and reviving a spiritually dead society.

Another basic requirement for starting was some idea of curriculum. What should they teach and why? They had the opportunity to start with a clean sheet and to ask the Lord for his approach. At about this time, Tim was very impressed by the opening verses of Psalm 78.

O my people, listen to my teaching, open your ears to what I am saying,
for I will speak to you in a parable.
I will teach you hidden lessons from our past – stories we heard and know,
Stories our ancestors handed down to us.
We will not hide these truths from our children but will tell the next generation about the glorious deeds of the Lord.
We will tell of his power and the mighty miracles he did.
For he issued his decree to Jacob; he gave his law to Israel.
He commanded our ancestors to teach them to their children,
So the next generation might know them – even the children not yet born – that they in turn might teach their children.
So each generation can set its hope anew on God,
remembering his glorious miracles and obeying his commands.
Then they will not be like their ancestors – stubborn, rebellious and unfaithful, refusing to give their hearts to God.

Through studying these verses, Tim became convinced that there should be two main themes at the core of their curriculum, a knowledge of God's activity in history and a thorough grounding in the principles of the word of God. As he thought about this further, he felt God highlight five key commandments and five areas that flowed from them.

The first was *'You shall love the Lord your God with all your heart, soul, mind and strength.'* They would need to provide opportunities for children to know God, to know about him and to serve him. They called this area 'Communion'.

The second area follows on. *'... and you shall love your neighbour as yourself.'* The children would need to understand relationships, the foundations of community life in family, church and state and so on. This was to be called 'Community study'.

The third area was 'Creation study' following from the command to mankind to fill the earth and subdue it.

The fourth command was based on the commission Jesus gave to his disciples to preach and to teach and would be called 'Communication'.

Finally, we are told that we must honour God with our bodies; hence the fifth area would be physical education.

These topics or headings gave a Biblical framework for subjects that are taught in most schools. It was not a case of finding a whole new set of topics, so much as finding the Biblical foundation for any particular sphere of knowledge and presenting the subject from that viewpoint. It would depend crucially on the teacher prayerfully approaching any and every subject from a Godly, Biblical and spiritual angle.

More faith needed!

By January 1986 all the legal paperwork was completed, and Oakfield House was owned by the school's Trust. In the months that followed, the lodge was sold, and the trustee provided the necessary additional sum. By October of that year, the school was very nearly free of debt to the Council. Just as things were settling down nicely, a bombshell arrived. Cleveland House was back on the market, the owners had found somewhere to move to and needed to move quickly. Could The River School, if they were still interested, exchange contracts the next day and complete a week later?

The school had always retained a sense that God was guiding them to this property, so Tim phoned all the trustees and asked them to pray. They all felt that the Lord wanted them to proceed. They had enough money to complete the sale on Oakfield House and enough to place the deposit on Cleveland House. This left them with the need to raise £60,000 in one week. It was half-term and everyone seemed to have gone away. Tim met with one of the others every day for prayer. By Thursday a major gift of £30,000 had been received. They had 24 hours to find the same amount again. Tim spoke to the school's bankers, and they agreed a loan of £30,000. Suddenly they were the owners of two properties! The new building was about 15 metres from a small brook and so it was decided to continue the image of the river and call it the Brook School. In January 1987, the Brook School opened, housing a small playgroup, a work that would later develop and expand.

A time of growth

The school was now blessed with two excellent properties and a time of growth and stability followed. Having begun in 1985 with 35 pupils, by the summer of 1986 the school numbered ninety. The Brook School eventually came to house the nursery and infant years, with juniors and secondary age children enjoying the facilities at the River School building. As the years passed, numbers eventually reached 170 and the school began to display the kind of success that is so typical of the new Christian schools. Now approaching almost twenty years of operation, the River and Brook Schools can testify to amazing stories of provision and to their desire to continue to learn how best to serve the children God has sent them.

Miracles on the Ski Slopes

Every two years, the River School organise a skiing trip for their older pupils. A group of about 25 pupils, accompanied by five members of staff, will visit the Alps and learn to ski. The first trip was held in 1989 but it was in 1991 at Imst in Austria that the excitement of skiing was put in the shade by a series of miraculous healings.

The trip that year was led by Graham Coyle, who in later years would become Tim Crow's successor as the school's headteacher. It was while the group were getting ready for their evening's activity on the first full day that the first accident happened. Paul, one of the older pupils, tripped on the stairs and injured his ankle very badly. He could not put his foot to the ground and a physiotherapist who was present warned that he would not be able to ski for the rest of the week.

Graham was very concerned for Paul, knowing how hard he had worked to save money for the trip. Later that evening, he asked if Paul believed that God could heal in answer to prayer. Paul replied that he did believe this. Graham, another member of staff and one of Paul's friends began to pray for him. They prayed for ten minutes that he would be healed. At the end of this time, nothing had happened. They prayed for a further ten minutes. Paul felt that perhaps his foot was a little better, but he still could hardly bear to put it to the ground. After another ten minutes of prayer the miracle happened – Paul was completely healed! He immediately ran up and down the stairs in great excitement at what had just occurred and was able to ski for the rest of the week as though there had never been an injury.

The next day, three minor injuries occurred amongst the group. In the light of what had happened the night before, all three were prayed for and all three were instantly healed.

It was the following day, on the ski slopes, that a more serious accident occurred. One of the girls, Anna, had wrenched her knee very badly and was in agony. Paramedics who were present strapped her to a sled and called an ambulance. By the time they had taken the sled down the slopes, the ambulance had arrived and she was taken to hospital. Graham went with her. A difficult time at the hospital followed. Anna was still in great pain, her knee was by this time enormously swollen and no-one seemed to be able to speak English. After examining her knee, the hospital staff strapped it up and sent her back to the hotel to rest. Graham returned to the ski slopes to join the rest of the group.

Arriving back at the slopes, Graham was greeted with news that he could hardly believe. There had been yet another accident, apparently even more serious. A young boy, Marcus, had been taken to hospital by helicopter, having fallen badly and landed on his head! His symptoms were worrying.

After they had all returned to the hotel, Graham was crying out to the Lord in desperation. Anna was in bed, still in great pain. Marcus was in hospital. It was the children who asked if they could go to Anna's room and pray for her. They had seen prayer answered and believed that God could do it again. Anna was willing to be prayed for, so under Graham's supervision, fifteen children crowded into her room and prayed for her. Within ten minutes, her knee was totally healed. Both the pain and the swelling had completely gone. The children also prayed for Marcus and within a short time he too had completely recovered and was back with them.

When the group of pupils and their teachers returned to Worcester, all that the children wanted to talk about was the healings that they had seen. For weeks it was their main topic of conversation and they were very eager to pray for anybody in need.

Since then, there have never been any serious accidents on the ski trips!

What do former pupils say?

'I loved the way it was not like any other kind of school – the teachers were more like friends than teachers. The atmosphere was very relaxed and yet we still worked quite hard. It was very exciting being there from the beginning and feeling, even as a pupil of eleven, part of the vision of the school, being involved in praying for deposits and mortgage payments and seeing them arrive.'

'I count it a privilege to have been a pupil at the school. I had regular first-hand experience of the reality of a God who loves and provides for his children.'

'At the time, I do not think I appreciated the River School fully. Looking back, I feel it gave me the opportunities and personality to achieve what I have today.'

'I am the teacher I am today because of my experiences as a pupil at the River School. The River School has had a huge impact on my life and career.'

'I started the River School hating everyone, feeling messed up from family troubles and I left with a firm foundation in the love of Christ. So, it was a privilege being a student at the River School and I would not consider anywhere else to send my children.'

Reverence for the LORD is the foundation of true wisdom. The rewards of wisdom come to all who obey him (Ps. 111:10).

> *'I will kill or cure: I will have one or the other, a Christian school, or none at all.'*
> From John Wesley's Journal, 12 March 1766.

10

The King's School, Nottingham

In 1985, church leaders at the Christian Centre and Clifton Christian Fellowship, two linked churches in Nottingham, became aware that all was not well with some of the school-age children who were part of their church community. The problems were so bad that, in some cases, parents were removing their children from the local schools. In one instance, a young girl had been making a stand for her Christian faith, only to find that her teachers mocked her for doing so. In another, the particular school concerned was not able to be flexible with a pupil with health problems. In other cases, parents recognised the strongly humanistic content of the education that their children were receiving and felt very unhappy with it.

As it happened, God had already spoken to the church leaders, particularly through verses in Deuteronomy 6, about the importance of a consistently Christian upbringing for the children of believers, and of the churches' responsibility to help them with this. Consequently, The King's School opened in

September 1986, with 65 children covering the age range from reception to Year 10.

During that first year, the school would only accept pupils from families who were members of the two founding fellowships. In accordance with a previously agreed plan, the following year, they widened their admissions policy to include all Christians and the third year extended it still further to include non-Christians as well. Rob Southey was appointed as the school's first Head teacher and, eighteen years and hundreds of pupils later, he remains in that position.

The school's prospectus contains the following brief description:

> The School seeks to promote good standards of discipline, behaviour and respect for authority. Warmth, firmness, forgiveness, consistency and truthfulness are held up as virtues and contribute to the standards of excellence expected in the life of the school. Children are taught in an atmosphere of Christian love, with Christian teachers committed to the development of the whole child.
>
> The King's School is enjoying a growing reputation for producing well-balanced, confident individuals. This is confirmed by the recognition of a number of Nottinghamshire's foremost sixth-form colleges, who welcome application from pupils of The King's School.

The school summarises its aims in the shape of the cross:

Seniors

To love God
and love one
another as
oneself

**"They that know their God shall
be strong and do exploits"**

Juniors

To know God,
becoming
more like
him

Infants

To know God
through His
word and
His creation

The prospectus also carries a message from well-known politician, Baroness Cox.

In recent years a number of new Christian schools have opened. Parents and teachers are seeking to provide an education in which children are valued as individuals and helped to develop their potential to fulfil God's plan for them. These schools provide spiritual, moral, intellectual and physical education within a caring, loving community. The King's School, Nottingham, is an excellent example of this new movement of Christian schools.

I pray that the school, and others like it, will flourish and continue to provide our young people with the most precious gifts of all: faith, hope and love.

We, as a nation, have been guilty of bringing up a generation ignorant of Christianity and cynical about spiritual matters. May God bless The King's School as they seek to remedy this failure by offering an education in which young people have the opportunity to learn about our Christian heritage and to experience the joy of worship in the community of faith.

Fear of the LORD is the beginning of wisdom. Knowledge of the Holy One results in understanding (Prov. 9:10).

> *'I preached on the education of children, wherein we are so shamefully wanting. Many were now deeply convinced of this. I hope they will not stifle all that conviction.'*
> From John Wesley's Journal, 30 November 1766.

11

Against all the Odds

Bethany School, Sheffield

At the end of their first year of operation, in July 1988, Bethany School very nearly closed. Another tiny, fragile Christian school looked as though it was about to be snuffed out. By all human reasoning, this should have been the end. It looked as if the school would finish the year with a big financial deficit. The rent for their building was suddenly doubled, putting those premises beyond their means. Then, to crown it all, the Lord called their one and only teacher, the one who had had the vision to pioneer the school, to move on to other things. No money, no premises, no teacher – it seemed impossible for the school to continue, but it never did close, and fifteen years later it is flourishing. How did it all come about?

Bethany School was founded in 1987 through the inspiration and vision of Steve Richards. In 1986, he had moved up from the south to teach at an independent school in Sheffield. While waiting to be able to move his family up to join him, he lodged with the Walze family. On the day Steve arrived, Ken Walze and his family could have had no idea of how profoundly this house guest was eventually going to alter their lives!

Steve shared with Ken and others about the Christian schools that he had seen begin to operate in the south. Gradually, several families became interested in providing a Christ-centred education for their children. After a public meeting was held, five families committed themselves to pioneering a Christian school. They rented a large room in the basement of the local YMCA and in September 1987, Bethany School opened with eleven children aged from four to eleven years. The eleven included four year old quads! Steve Richards became the teacher, with some parental help.

A big crisis
At the end of that first year, Bethany School had the encouragement of fifteen children on the books for the following September. However, they had lost their main teacher and their premises and were facing the prospect of financial deficit. Undeterred, the embryonic school moved into the cramped, damp basement of a tiny church. With no main teacher, the education was provided by the children's mothers, with help and advice from qualified teachers, particularly Ken Walze, who was beginning to play a leading role in co-ordinating the teaching at the school.

After half a term, conditions improved. The school moved to the basement of the nearby Sharrowvale Methodist church. When the time to move came, the children and their mothers picked up everything and walked round the corner to the new premises! Help came on the teaching front, too, in the form of Kathy Chambers who was employed part-time to help the Mums. After Christmas, she became full-time.

Further developments
By the beginning of the following school year, Bethany's third, the school had its first secondary-aged children. Kathy was

successfully establishing the primary part of the school, but who would teach these older children? Ken decided to take two terms leave of absence – unpaid leave – from his teaching position, so that he could work voluntarily in the school and try to get it established.

Meanwhile the Bethany team were doing all that they could to acquire extra resources for their new premises. Early one morning they heard that a large quantity of redundant toy equipment was in the process of being burnt. They rushed to the scene and rescued what they could from the flames! The school was now the proud owner of a big supply of plastic frogs and tiddlywinks and it was amazing how creative they became in finding uses for them!

A happy time
The three years that the school spent at Sharrowvale were happy and stable. After Ken's two terms were over, he applied for one more year of absence and the school started to pay him a little although he needed to drive a lorry for one day a week to help with finances. By Easter of that year, Ken had written to resign from his former job and he has stayed at Bethany ever since.

At Sharrowvale, there was a sense that the school was flourishing, albeit that everything was still on a small scale. The children were all taught in one room under an 'open plan' arrangement, they produced excellent work and there was a steady increase in the number of families giving sacrificially to the school, both in terms of money and time. As with so many of the new Christian schools, members of staff were working for very low salaries to make the project possible.

The problems of growth
As the numbers at the school grew, so too did numbers at the church in whose building they were housed. It became

apparent that the church would soon require their basement back. Bethany were on the lookout for new premises and were told that a big old Methodist church building in Anns Road had just come on to the market. The school investigated this possibility, but as the building was quite large and was in good condition, the asking price was far outside their range. They had heard that the new Sheffield Chinese Christian Church was looking for a property to buy, so they informed them of the Anns Road possibility. The Chinese Church subsequently went ahead with the purchase.

Bethany School were continuing to look and pray for alternative premises for themselves when to their great surprise they received an offer from the Chinese Church. They were invited to share the Anns Road premises with the Chinese Church, rent free, for two years to give them time to find somewhere else! The church would use the worship area, the school could use the upstairs accommodation and the two groups would share the large downstairs room.

From the start, Bethany were looking for their own building, knowing that the offer from the Chinese Church was only temporary. The two years that had been offered did not prove to be enough and in the end Bethany shared the premises of the Chinese Church for a full ten years. Throughout that time, the Chinese Church served the Christian School in a quiet, supportive, sacrificial way without one cross word.

Up and down years at the Chinese Church

Now that they were in larger premises, Bethany School was able to grow to more than sixty pupils. The growth brought its own problems as some families came to join who proved to want something different from the school's strong Christian vision. Perhaps they were attracted by the excellent examination results that the school was now achieving. As these problems were ironed out, families would sometimes leave and numbers would drop again. New families would soon come forward to replace those who had left.

Throughout this phase, the running of the school was still based on sacrifice and service, with volunteers giving much time to the school. During the whole ten years, the school was actively seeking new premises. A building fund was established which grew to contain about £80,000. Ten different properties were extensively investigated. In three cases the properties were surveyed and planning applications were made, but all came to nothing. It seemed that the school simply had not yet found the Lord's place for them.

A new home for Bethany School!

On Monday 2nd April 2001 at 5 p.m. the school received a telephone call. It came from a representative of the Chinese Church who was calling to explain that their work was expanding and they now needed full use of their premises. Would it be possible for the school to vacate the building by September?

A joint staff and governors' meeting was already scheduled for 9.30 p.m. that evening. It went ahead as planned. The main item on the agenda was the School Development Plan, but discussion ended prematurely when they ran out of things to say! The meeting resorted to prayer.

On Tuesday 10th April, in the evening, the Bethany School Building Committee met to discuss options. They decided to scour estate agents, ring the City Council, contact Diocesan property agents, inform the local media, tour the streets and keep on praying!

The breakthrough came on Friday 27th April at 4.15 p.m. in the form of a telephone call from agents for the Sheffield Diocese. Would Bethany be interested in the former St.

Stephen's School? Would they! After inspection of the property had proved satisfactory, the Building Committee met with the agents on May 10th. It was agreed that, in deciding what amount to offer, the School could subtract their legal costs, removal expenses and essential building work costs from their £80,000 building fund. On 18th May, the agents phoned the school to confirm the sale. After ten years of prayer and effort, when the right building was finally located everything was agreed in less than a month and in time to comply with the needs of the Chinese Church.

Over that summer of 2001, there was much activity as parents and friends of the school worked to get the building ready for opening. High quality furniture and equipment was provided at just the right time, for a nominal charge of £50, from a local hospital which was moving into different premises. In September 2001, 60 excited children moved into their new school home.

What of the future?
Since moving to their permanent home, Bethany School has seen an increase in the number of their pupils. However, they do not wish to grow much bigger than 100, believing in the value of operating as a small family school. Instead, they would like to pioneer the development of a network of small Christian schools, like theirs is, all around Sheffield. It remains to be seen if this vision will be realised, but one thing is certain. If God intends to do it, it will happen at the right time. That is the enduring testimony of Bethany School – God has sent them everything they need at the right time. From tiddlywinks to people to buildings – all provided at just the right time.

What do former pupils say?
'I really enjoyed school and have never once regretted the

fact that I went to a Christian School. I think that it gave me a very good education and also a good grounding in Christian teaching and values. I felt valued and cared for as an individual, in contrast to most of my experiences in further education. I would love to teach in a Christian school. Since I am training as a teacher, I have had some experience of state schools and have therefore been able to compare my experiences and have realised the benefits of Christian schools.'

'I feel that attending a Christian School not only gave me a better academic background, but also prepared me as a person and as a Christian for the rest of my life and I have never felt I lacked anything in comparison with friends from state schools. In fact, the more I compare myself and others from Bethany with people from state schools, the more I realise what a privilege I had in going to Bethany.'

And now a word to you fathers. Don't make your children angry by the way you treat them. Rather, bring them up with the discipline and instruction approved by the Lord (Eph. 6:4).

'Pay the utmost attention to the schools. I consider schools as one of the most effectual means of spreading the light of the gospel through the world.'
William Carey in a letter to Jabez Carey 1815.

12

Christ the King School, Sale, Cheshire

Christ the King School was founded by South Manchester Christian Fellowship in September 1988. It was born out of the desire of a number of Christian parents to provide an education that was based on the fact that God exists, that he created everything and that he wants to be involved in all aspects of our lives.

Their vision statement:
Young people loving Christ Jesus with all their heart, soul and strength.

Their mission statement:
Christ the King serves the parents and members of South Manchester Christian Fellowship in developing a Christ-like intellect and character within young people, so that they may be released into the full measure of their God-given potential and fulfil God's plan for themselves and His creation.

What some past pupils say:

'At times it was easy to look at other children at other schools and want to be part of that, but towards the end in particular, and certainly with hindsight, I wouldn't change it for the world! I think the school was an excellent foundation for me to build my life on, as I have gained understanding of the Bible and moral principles that many don't have the opportunity to at such a young age. Looking at the people from my year group and comparing them with those in the same year from other schools (even Christians), I can see a wisdom that many others don't yet have. Spiritually, I felt it matured us earlier and I am so grateful for that opportunity.'

'I am very grateful to my parents for sending me to Christ the King. They believed it was a worthwhile investment and I am now reaping the benefits. I would always want my children to go to a school like mine, where there is a real family environment.

Through the years I had a lot of input from the school and when I went to sixth form I was able to put it into practice. That's when I felt really passionate about Christian education, because I could see how much it had helped.'

Whatever you eat or drink or whatever you do, you must do it all for the glory of God (1 Cor. 10:31).

> *'The philosophy of the classroom is the philosophy of the Government in the next generation.'*
> Abraham Lincoln

13

A '*Light for the World*' in Northern Ireland
Kingsland School, Bangor

The seaside town of Bangor was once known as 'the light of the world' because of its spiritual and educational significance. Now, in a very enviable location, right beside the seashore, stands another light for education. As the children of Kingsland School look out from their classroom, they are looking across the bay from where, 1500 years ago, countless missionaries sailed, travelling in groups of twelve, to carry the gospel to Britain and Europe. In the Bangor monastery, Christian monks were discipled in worship, the word of God, mission and the highest standards of education available at the time. From the 6th to the 11th centuries, they were the educators of Europe.

'For them, worship, mission and education were a seamless garment and this has always been an inspiration to us,' says John Kelly, a medically qualified doctor and pastor who is now school principal. John has a deep sense of Christian history. He draws strength from the stories of Congall, Columbus and Gall, outstanding missionaries and educators who planted several schools throughout Britain and Europe. These schools offered an enlightened curriculum of Hebrew, Latin, Greek, astronomy, science, literature, maths and agriculture. John's vision is a committed and passionate one and he is following in their footsteps to offer radical approaches to curriculum at Kingsland School.

How did it all start?

John's vision for Christian education was first ignited when he saw Christian schools in operation in the USA. 'I realised for the first time that it was possible to offer a curriculum and teaching approach that was thoroughly Biblical,' says John. At the time, his daughter, Sarah, was aged three and was attending a church playgroup. John and his wife Barbara decided that rather than send her to a state school, they would educate her at home. Sadly, Barbara died suddenly in 1988 and John had to make a difficult decision: should he continue with the plan to home school, or not?

By this time, contact had been made with David Freeman, principal of The King's School, Witney. He offered to support John by providing curriculum and advice. Several other church families followed John's courageous example and it was decided to open a parent-controlled school, using church premises. The elders of the church supported their vision, but there was resistance from a significant number of church members. This was perhaps due, in part, to the unique educational attitudes of Northern Ireland, which find particularly strong expression in Bangor.

Darkening Clouds

The fledgling school began in a climate where there is a well-respected monolithic education system with very wide cultural diversity. Roman Catholics have their own schools and most other state schools are Protestant. As a Protestant or a Catholic, you send your child to the appropriate school. An alternative non-denominational Christian school like Kingsland was unheard of. With a strong percentage of evangelical teachers in the state schools and high standards, both academically and morally, the question was asked, 'Why open another type of school? What is the point?'

John, the parents and the future staff were assailed by doubts in those early days. Nevertheless, the school opened in 1989 with 15 pupils aged 4–7 years and one courageous and gifted teacher, Susan Johnston, who taught four year groups in one class! 'Are we stupid?' they asked themselves and as many discouragements came, the doubts continued. Each June, they wondered if the school would still be open the following September, but in fact the school grew and by 1991 there were 45 pupils with two full-time and two part-time teachers.

John, the staff and parents drew encouragement from their contact with the school at Witney. 'Links with David and the staff there have been a life-saver for us,' says John, 'Seeing them win their battles has helped us to press on through.

'The darkness shall not overcome it'
In those early years there was much to press on through. There were serious health problems for some members of the school community, including John's own exhausting battle with ME. More discouragement came in 1997–9, as numbers dropped to 20, causing increased financial pressures. God challenged John to pray and believe that 10 pupils would be added each year. The children joined him in praying consistently and their faith has been rewarded as numbers have steadily risen again to reach the present 50. 'The prayers of our children have been an important part of the school's growth,' John reflects warmly.

Creative tension

The 11+ examination still operates in Bangor and tremendous pressure is placed on primary-aged pupils as it approaches. Pupils who do not make the grade and are therefore unable to transfer to the Grammar School tend to be regarded as failures, even though they may have tried their very best. John knows that this scenario is at odds with the philosophy of Christian education, which values every individual regardless of academic ability. He says, 'We have been successful at enabling children to achieve academic results at an appropriate level and have had good results in the transfer exam, yet our main commitment has been not to let that dominate our teaching styles.'

In October 2001, John heard the Lord ask him to take the school on to secondary level. He and his team, headed by Cathy Frame, responded to this call and in September 2002 Kingsland proudly opened its Middle School.

Throughout all the trials and difficulties, John and the rest of the school community have been strengthened by the words of Psalm 127. They know that '*Unless the Lord builds the house, its builders labour in vain.*' The psalm goes on to say that children are a reward from the Lord and are like arrows in the hands of a warrior, whose parents will not be put to shame. Kingsland School believe that they are seeing these promises fulfilled.

Come, my children, and listen to me, and I will teach you to fear the Lord (Ps. 34:11).

14

Churches Unite

Bradford Christian School

The beginnings

Phil and Audrey Moon were married in 1983. They went into marriage with a great sense of expectation that God had plans for their lives and they began, right from the start, to seek to know what these were. They were both teachers in Bradford and were determined, for the Lord's sake, to be the very best teachers that they could be, but it wasn't until their own children were born between 1984 and 1987 that they began to think about education from a radical and Christian perspective. They began to realise that in order to maintain the intimate and real relationship with God that they were experiencing as a family, the schooling of their children would need to involve the Lord as well.

By 1992, Phil was a deputy head teacher in a middle school, and at times during that year he was acting head teacher. This gave him great insights into how a school should be run. It was during that year, also, that God brought him together with Paul Cribb. Paul shared Phil and Audrey's vision for a Christian school in Bradford and was willing to support their efforts to start one. Phil and Paul presented their vision for a school to the eldership of their own church, Church on the Way. The elders encouraged them to get wider support from the Christian community and so began a year of visiting many local churches with the message of Christian education. Not all of the meetings were very encouraging or inspiring. On one occasion, a cold, snowy winter's night, there were just six people present in a draughty church hall for the meeting, two of whom were Phil and Paul!

Nevertheless, by the end of that year, a small group of men from a number of different churches had agreed to become founding governors of the as yet non-existent school. In May 1993, this group realised that a decision needed to be made. Could they start the school the following September? If they decided to do so, Phil would need to hand in his notice by May 31st. They carefully weighed up the facts. They had 17 children committed to the project and £4,000 raised towards the £60,000 that they reckoned would be needed, but no premises. From a human point of view, it did not seem sensible to proceed.

Prayer and faith

The thought of the major steps of faith that would need to be made drove Phil and the others to earnest prayer. As they prayed, the Lord seemed to increase their faith. Phil handed in his resignation, and everyone concerned had a sense that they were stepping out into the unknown. Phil himself was faced with the task of explaining to his parents why he had given up a great job with excellent prospects and a good salary, and just how he was going to provide for his family of a wife and three children under the age of nine. The day that the family were due to travel down to see Phil's parents, two envelopes arrived. One contained a cheque for £10,000, a real encouragement for the whole family that God would provide. The other envelope was just as encouraging in its own way. It contained a 50p piece, together with a simple note from a girl who was due to start at the school. 'This is half my pocket money, but you can have all of it.'

Three months later, with 44 children and the full £60,000 raised, Bradford Christian School opened.

The fledgling school matures

In 1993 there were just two classes covering Reception to Year 6. Another class was added each year for the next five years. The school's premises consisted mainly of several portakabin classrooms on a site shared with a developing church. By 1998, numbers at the school had grown to 150 and unsuccessful attempts had been made to find better premises. It seemed that they were destined to spend their existence crammed into overworked facilities. A number of offers were made on buildings in the local area, including a £750,000 bid for a local school. In this they were outbid by a local businessman. It seemed to the school that theirs was a story of disappointment yet of continually looking for provision.

During the summer of 2001, the wife of the chairman of the governors was staying in a Brazilian hotel overlooking a beach. A stream which had its origins in the surrounding hillside ran along the beach. During the night, a torrential storm turned the stream into a great gorge. As she reflected on this occurrence and prayed over the fate of the school, she felt God say to her that he could act just as quickly and decisively when he chose to.

Phil felt encouraged when he heard this story, and sure enough it was not long before the Lord began to act.

A new building

The school team became aware of a 1.2 acre site containing a school building and a generous playground. The building was one of the first built by the government in 1876 in response to the 1872 Forster Education Act which made it the responsibility of the state to provide for education. They made an offer of £100,000 for this building during the week before Christmas 2001. The offer was accepted and just a month later the school took possession of the keys.

It was obvious that the building was going to need a lot of refurbishment before it was ready for the children to move in. As soon as the school had gained possession of the building, a parent whose eldest child had just started as a pupil came forward and offered his services. Phil Wells was prepared to give up his job as a high-class shopfitter and undertake the necessary renovations. His skills and expertise made him ideally suited to reclaim and restore the building. Over the next three months, Phil, his labourer William, together with many volunteers managed to transform the site. The older half of the school was able to move in during April 2002 and the younger half joined them the following November.

God's provision of the building together with the means of transforming it, the fact that it all happened so quickly and the beautiful result had the effect of taking everyone's breath away and of renewing their confidence in the Lord. Another result of having the extra space was a rapid growth in numbers of the school population to 200.

Project Romania

For many years, Phil and his team had a desire to take some of the young people abroad as part of their school experience. Rather than visit another rich European country as tourists, they wanted to visit a poorer country, where they might work alongside Christian missionaries. They prayed and talked to various missionaries who visited the school on home leave.

At Christmas in 1998, the Moons got the opportunity as a family to visit orphanages in Bucharest. This led to a return trip the following summer with a small group of students to work with a church in Bucharest. While there, Phil heard about a young Brazilian missionary who had just started a Christian ministry in Mangalia, a seaside town on the shores of the Black Sea. He hitched a ride there with a van load of supplies and spent an evening with the missionary, Ireni De Silva. They soon realised that God was calling them to work together and the school now sends groups of pupils to support Ireni each summer. They assist her in her work with the Amadeus Foundation, a health project dedicated to helping poor Romanian families with their newborn babies.

Many of the students who take part in the project report that they have had life-changing experiences as a result. They invariably want to return the next year. A local church involved with the school has purchased a flat in Mangalia which sleeps fourteen people, thus making it easier to cater for the trips. Two former pupils from the school have spent their gap years serving in the project. Students have come to know Jesus for the first time on these visits and many have had a taste of what it means to serve God and give one's life over to his will and purposes.

A provision of people
Sometimes staff are provided in almost miraculous ways. One year, with only ten days to go before the end of the summer term, the school was still desperately seeking a replacement science teacher for the following September. Unexpectedly, in the post came a newsletter from an acquaintance, someone Phil had not seen for eight years. After a speculative phone

call, the potential teacher visited, returned with his family and decided to join the school. This gave him seven weeks to settle his affairs, sell his house, find a new one and move his family up from Sussex to Bradford. Amazingly, this is exactly what happened.

Grateful hearts

Bradford Christian School is so grateful for all that God has done for them in providing for them and in answering prayer. They are grateful, too, for the opportunity to fulfil the Biblical mandate to work with parents in the bringing up of their children. They do not take for granted the freedom that they have to work with children, young people and their families in the environment of a Christian school. Their desire is to introduce the children to the inspiring character of God as Saviour, Father, Creator and friend. The children are growing up seeing the regular and varied provision of a mighty God and the hope is that they will never forget what they have seen of God's power and faithfulness in action.

An amazing story

At the end of our first year in the life of the school, our three children, then aged 9, 8 and 6 came into our bedroom and asked if we could all go to the cinema on the first day of the holidays. Having taken a big drop in our previous salaries, money was tight, but Mum said we could pray about it. So we sat all together on the bedspread and told Father God that we would like to go to the cinema together. As we finished praying, the postman arrived and we heard some letters drop on to the mat. When we opened the letters, one contained five cinema tickets from a friend of the school.

Talk about timing, talk about provision, talk about the blessing of a father-hearted God!

We had a great time that afternoon, watching the new Flintstones movie ... though I don't suppose three little boys really understood why Mum and Dad kept crying on such a fabulous treat!

Phil Moon

The 'Culture' of Bradford Christian School

Phil asked some Year 9 pupils who had attended other schools to evaluate the culture that they found at the Christian school. It was agreed that there were some ways in which behaviour could be improved and the school determined to work hard on these.

However, the students wanted to make the following observations about what they had found at the Christian school.

You can do your work
There is much less bullying
There is little or no vandalism
Behaviour is much better
There is less peer pressure
You feel safe
There is no physical threat
People generally respect property
People are more polite
There is no smoking
There are no drugs

How wonderful it is, how pleasant, when brothers live together in harmony! (Ps. 133:1).

> *'Your ministry embraces two things. The establishment of schools and the spread of the gospel. The first of these if it can be secured will I trust be an effectual introduction to the other.'*
> William Carey in a letter to Jabez Carey, 1819

15

The Making of a Gem ... by faith!

Chrysolyte School, London

Two Nigerians, one a former Moslem, with limited resources have ended up owning and running a Christian School in Central London with 110 Afro-Caribbean pupils. It is a startling demonstration of faith in action.

Joseph and Rally Ikiebe's story begins when they arrived in England in 1984. Within four years they had had an encounter with Jesus Christ, which changed their lives. God began to challenge them about the need for a Christian education for their three children. Rally therefore began to educate them, together with a neighbour's two children, in her own home after school and on Saturdays. Meanwhile, Joseph, in studying the Bible had a growing sense of compassion for the Afro-Caribbean families in their community. The Saturday school seemed to meet a need and rapidly grew to 60, moving to bigger and bigger halls. Parents encouraged them to start a 'proper' school – something they had not thought of! By 1993 they were praying and fasting weekly to be sure that God wanted them to do this. Meanwhile, the problems they saw afflicting the community families around them spurred them on.

Signed and sealed

The hunt for property began. Offers of finance came to nothing until one day Rally felt prompted to pray first and then call the landlord of a large house in the area. Within a month everything was signed and sealed and on January 9th 1995 Chrysolyte School opened, in a basement floor, with only six children! By the end of the year they were thirty-five strong.

Where did such an unusual name come from? Joseph felt that God drew his attention to a verse in the last book of the Bible mentioning foundational gemstones. One of these, the chrysolyte, is yellow, green and brown. Joseph felt that God was saying that their children would become foundation stones for good in society and those colours are now the colours of their uniform.

Failure and success

May 1995 brought an official inspection. Although the Inspector was very helpful he said he could not accept their school; it would take four years for their standards to be raised to acceptable levels. They worked hard to fulfil every one of his recommendations and, much to his surprise he was able to officially recommend them the following year!

'I can't believe this is the same school', he said in amazement.

A broader place

The next challenge was that they were beginning to outgrow the premises. At the same time the owner began to make life difficult by obstructing them and causing impossible noise. Each time Joseph walked through the basement corridors he felt an increasing sense of choking restrictions.

As Joseph prayed, a promise became clear: there was a 'broader place'. He followed up one property after another and visited several London boroughs to pray in them. Nothing seemed to be the right place, but great encouragement came when a parent felt God tell her to inform Joseph: 'God has given you a property – it is in Southwark – between New Cross and The Elephant and Castle'. A big library in Southwark came up for sale and fell through, as did other properties in the same borough. In the summer of 1998 Joseph began to get more passionate and determined in prayer. He reminded God of the families in the community who needed his touch. After that, things became even more difficult. Parents of the school children got really worried and began to doubt the school would ever move. The landlord of the school property became even more difficult and increased the rent by 25%. One parent offered a building, but Joseph felt that he must not accept anything that did not fit the description that God had revealed.

The roller coaster of faith!

In November 1999 Joseph, Rally, and the school began a month of prayer and fasting. On the very first day Rally had a phone call from a parent who had seen a 'For Sale' sign displayed on Lansdowne Medical Mission Centre, owned by the Shaftesbury Society. Where was it positioned? Yes, it was in Southwark between New Cross and The Elephant and Castle!

However, there was only one problem. Offers were requested in excess of £200,000 and Joseph and Rally had only £25,000 in the bank. By faith they offered £250,000 but suddenly, wealthy companies began to offer a million pounds! There were sixteen similar bidders, so Joseph and Rally's meagre offer was not even acknowledged. Rally felt she should write to the Director of the Shaftesbury Society, but he said the property must go to the highest bidder.

From November to March there was five months of silence to be endured, but Joseph and Rally continued to pray. Joseph led them to pray at the building every week. Out of the blue there came a phone call from the estate agent saying: "If you're still interested you need to upgrade your offer.' It was now between them and just one other bidder!

Impossible odds
Joseph and Rally had less than £25,000 in the bank but by faith they upgraded their offer to £350,000. This was still too low. Finally, Rally felt God telling her to go to the estate agent again. When she got there, he said, 'I've never had to work as hard on any building as I have this one. The local council have refused all of the large bidders.'

Joseph and Rally were greatly encouraged. It seemed that all the time God had been working through the local council!

A month went by. The agent asked for their best and final offer as £350,000 was not enough! As they prayed God impressed on their minds, independently, the same huge figure – £500,000 – a half a million pounds. But they did not have this amount of money! Checking with a consultant they were assured this was what the building was worth. The bank would only lend 70%, so by faith, they felt they must go forward with this amazing offer. The agent required £100,000 as down-payment, but despite this daunting demand both Joseph and Rally felt even more strongly that God would have them go forward in faith. At this point their consultant reminded them that they had the equity on two small houses, one of which was purchased and one on a mortgage. By sacrificing their home they were able to raise a mortgage on the proposed site.

On 6th January 2001 seventy-three children and their teachers moved The Chrysolyte School into the historic Shaftesbury building. It had been the first 'ragged school', opened by Christians for the poor in the 19th Century.

The school is an island surrounded on all sides by blocks of flats housing the families for whom Joseph and Rally feel such compassion.

> *'Faith means putting our full confidence in the things we hope for, it means being certain of things we cannot see'* as the J B Phillips translation of Hebrews 11:1 says.

The Chrysolyte School is a lesson to us all of what can be achieved through persistent and active faith.

**And this is what God says to all humanity:
The fear of the Lord is true wisdom; to forsake
evil is real understanding (Job 28:28).**

16

Ask and you will receive

Emmaus School, Trowbridge, Wiltshire

Prayer prepares the way
In the early 1970s, some Christians in Bradford-on-Avon became concerned about the need for a Christian school in their area. In 1971 they held a public meeting with John Harding as the main speaker, but although some interest was generated, nothing concrete ever came of it. For some of them, however, the burden remained and they prayed through the years that God would eventually establish a school, even though by now it was too late for their own children to benefit from it. ˙

Prayer begins to receive an answer
In 1993, Miriam Wiltshire, who lived near Trowbridge, became concerned that her six year old daughter was unhappy at her state school. Both parents could see that the little girl was rapidly losing confidence. Miriam began to wonder if a Christian school might be the answer. She had heard of one in Oxford, Emmanuel School, and decided to pay it a visit. That visit had a profound effect on Miriam. The school seemed such a safe environment – exactly the kind of place that she would

want for her children. As she looked at the displays on the walls and saw the word of God featured prominently there, she realised that for a child at a school like this, there would be no conflict between what was taught in the home and what was taught in the school. Miriam herself had been brought up in a Christian home and her own education had set up tensions within her. The values and approaches of school and home had been so different – it had been very hard to cope with. She had resolved the problem by living two lives, thinking one way at home and differently at school. Miriam realised for the first time that this did not need to happen to her own children, if only they had a local Christian school.

A vision takes hold

The visit to Oxford had sparked off a deep interest in Christian education in Miriam. Over the next couple of years, she read anything on the subject that she could lay her hands on, and hoped and prayed that the Lord would give them a school.

Miriam had been very impressed with the way in which Emmanuel School in Oxford had been able to start. The small group that had wanted to open a school there had been given a huge boost by an unsolicited offer of financial assistance that had been given to them, out of the blue, just as they were making the final decision to go ahead. 'How wonderful to be given such a clear sign from God,' she thought, 'but I can't imagine how such a thing could ever happen to me!'

Something extraordinary happens

In 1996, completely unexpectedly, came the kind of sign from the Lord that Miriam thought only happened to other people. A local Victorian primary school came on to the market and an anonymous donor offered to loan Miriam and her husband Kevin the money to buy it! The sale was being conducted by closed bid, so Miriam and Kevin put in their offer, which was accepted. Later they found out that someone had in fact made a higher bid, but for some reason the decision was made to give the building to them. It seemed that the Lord did indeed want them to start a school! By November 1996, the building was theirs.

Where are the children?
Although there were no children in prospect for the school, other than their own, Miriam and Kevin were not deterred. The Lord had given them a building. Surely he was going to provide the teachers and pupils as well! As 1997 dawned, the couple approached some like-minded friends and asked them to join the governing body of the proposed school. Eventually a group of eight governors was busily at work planning a curriculum.

There were still no prospective pupils, but they did have a teacher in mind. Naomi Oliver was a local Christian primary teacher who seemed ideal for the job. She was interested in Christian education for a very good reason. Her father, Dr. Robert Oliver, had been part of that group in the 70s who had tried to get a school going. He had wanted such a school for Naomi and her brother and had been praying for one ever since!

It seemed an outrageous thing to do, to ask Naomi to resign from her job to take up a position in a non-existent school with no pupils, but that is exactly what the governing body did! Even more amazingly, Naomi immediately agreed to do it! When the approach came, although it was unexpected, she realised that God had been preparing her and knew for certain that this was his call.

So now there was a building and a teacher but still no pupils!

The step of faith

In June, everyone involved with the prospective school became convinced that it was necessary to move forward in faith and so the decision was made to open the school the following September. On 10th September 1997, Emmaus School opened with three full-time pupils, and one part-time. The name 'Emmaus' is taken from the famous incident recorded in Luke 24, when Jesus appeared after his resurrection to two disciples as they walked from Jerusalem to the village of Emmaus. As they walked together, Jesus himself instructed his followers and this is what the parents and teachers want for the children of Emmaus School as they journey through life.

Numbers of children have grown slowly but surely since the school began, and there are now three separate classes, covering the full age range from 5 to 16. For Dr. Robert Oliver there is particular joy in this situation. His many years of prayer have resulted in a Christian school in which his two children are both teachers and in which his four grandchildren are all registered! For Miriam Wiltshire too a dream has become a reality as she heads up a school of more than 30 pupils and five teachers.

Blessed are those who do not walk in the counsel of the wicked or stand in the way of sinners or sit in the seat of mockers. But their delight is in the law of the Lord, and on his law they meditate day and night. They are like trees planted by streams of water, which yield their fruit in season and whose leaves do not wither. Whatever they do prospers (Ps. 1:1-3).

George Muller is famous for his orphanages, founded in Bristol in the 19th century. Few people realise that he came to Bristol to establish Christian schools.

Scriptural Knowledge Society
Founded 5th March 1834

1. To assist Day-schools, Sunday-schools and Adult-schools, in which instruction is given upon Scriptural Principles, and, as far as the Lord may graciously give the means and supply us with suitable teachers, to establish Schools of this kind.

2. To put the children of poor persons to such Day-schools, in order that they may be truly instructed in the ways of God, besides learning those things which are necessary for this life.

(Signed George Muller and Henry Craik,
7th October 1834)

> *'Surely the importance of Kingswood School is apparent, even from the difficulties that attend it. I have spent more money, and time, and care on this, than almost any design I ever had.... But it is worth all the labour.'*
> From John Wesley's Journal, 24 August 1753.

17

Hebridean Miracle

Lewis Independent School, Stornoway, Western Isles

At the end of 1998, a public meeting was held on the Isle of Lewis to raise the possibility of the founding of a Christian school. There was considerable media hostility to this event. Nevertheless, a small number of interested parents prayerfully formed an executive committee and drew up a constitution. The desire for a Christian school on the island was growing and becoming more urgent, but practically the situation was very daunting. Funds were very low, and there was no building or teacher in sight. The prospects looked bleak.

By the spring of 1999, a teacher had been appointed, someone everyone agreed had been chosen for the task by the Lord. There were still no funds and no sign of a building, but the clear guidance that the committee had received as they had looked for a teacher had strengthened everyone's faith. While praying for premises, one of this pioneering group felt strongly directed towards a certain building. Enquiries were made and it was found that this building was prepared to house the school. A lease was drawn up. Progress was being made!

On 17th August 1999, Lewis Independent School opened

with a thanksgiving service, in temporary rooms. It seemed a miracle that they had actually been able to start! There were nine pupils ranging in age from five to ten years.

That first week saw God provide in amazing ways, honouring the steps of faith that had been taken. They had started the school employing a full-time teacher, renting temporary rooms, intending to lease another building for £5,000 per year, having ordered £400 worth of books, plus other expenses, with only £1,600 in the bank! The first day, they were handed £180. The following day a donation of £12,500 was received and on Thursday an additional £200. At the end of the week, after adding on Gift Aid, they had over £16,500 in the bank!

In the years that have followed that exciting beginning, the school has seen God at work many times, providing for them, leading them through trials and disappointments and increasing their vision for the future.

Wisdom is supreme; therefore get wisdom. Though it cost all you have get understanding (Prov. 4:7).

18

The Christian Schools' Trust

The stories that you have just read are representative of the approximately one hundred new Christian schools now operating in this country. Many of the others would give you similar accounts of faith, prayer, sacrifice and success following small beginnings. New schools continue to be opened.

Fifty or so of the schools are affiliated to the Christian Schools' Trust. In about 1982, several of the new schools became aware of the existence of the others and for the first time a number of the head teachers met together for discussion, prayer and mutual encouragement. Out of this, the Christian Schools' Trust was established to support the existing schools and to encourage the setting up of new ones.

A variety of schools

The schools are varied and diverse in approach and this is a strength of the movement. All are committed to being Christ-centred, to basing their teaching on biblical principles and to developing a Christian world-view. They range in size from a handful of pupils to more than two hundred. Some are primary schools; others cover the full age range from nursery to GCSE. A few have experimented with, or are pursuing, educating the 16-18 age group.

Some of the schools are closely linked to a particular church, others are supported by a variety of local churches while still others operate as parent co-operatives.

A common vision

Although they may display some differences, a very strong, common vision unites the schools – the need to make available a Christian alternative for the education of children. Those who have founded the schools have usually themselves been teachers in secular schools, be they state run or part of the private sector. They have been able to observe first-hand a non-Christian philosophy of life being promoted in the classroom and underlying the basis of everything that is taught. This applies whether the pupil is aged four or fourteen; children are being educated to view life as though God does not exist, or as though he has no relevance to what is being taught. Those who are running the schools believe that Christianity affects the whole of life and that there is a Christian perspective on every academic subject.

In addition to the content of the lessons, the schools are united in wanting a Christian ethos within which the children can be educated, similar to one that would be found in a Christian home. Only a Christian can truly be *in loco parentis* for a child from a Christian home. The academic knowledge and teaching ability of the teacher are not the only criteria; the schools want all those involved in the education of the children to be living by Christian principles and to display Christian attitudes. They believe that teachers should pray for, and with, the children, just as Christian parents do.

A radically different curriculum

The schools are also united in believing that their curricula should be fundamentally different from other schools, covering much of the same material, perhaps, but from a very different viewpoint. The starting point should be the Lord himself and his truth. What would he want his children to learn from this particular subject or topic? Is the topic itself sufficiently important to be included in a Christian curriculum? Will it help the child to understand more about God, more about the nature of the fallen world we live in and more about how to live in a way that pleases God?

One fundamental difference setting the Christian schools apart is their understanding of the importance of wisdom and its relationship to knowledge. Whereas much of modern education is preoccupied with acquiring knowledge and skills, particularly that knowledge and those skills which would enable the child ultimately to make money in a technological society, wisdom is concerned with how we live. Knowledge is not just there to be acquired, but to be handled wisely, and, as the Bible says over and over again, the fear of the Lord is where wisdom begins.

Some subjects are a lot to do with acquiring skills and those involved with Christian education are often asked such questions as, 'But surely 2 + 2 = 4 whether you are a Christian or not. Surely there isn't a Christian approach to a subject like Maths?' In fact, the framework within which Maths is taught is fundamentally affected by the teacher's religious position. Number flows from the nature of God himself – he is three persons in one – and number is very important to God. There is even a book of the Bible called Numbers! Numbers have meaning and symbolism in the Bible. God is infinite and the inclusion of the concept of infinity is crucial to mathematics. These considerations should enable us to approach the subject with respect and with confidence. Humans are made in the image of God; therefore somewhere inside all of us is the ability to handle numbers. Added to this, Maths is the language of science, one of the main ways in which we can describe and understand the workings of God's creation. It is no coincidence that both the development of Maths and of modern science took enormous strides forward in Puritan England, at a time when the whole culture was soaked in a knowledge of the Bible and most people believed in God-ordained order and purpose in the Universe. It is also no coincidence that decades of teaching Maths in a culture that has lost those moorings has resulted in a crisis; so many children no longer seem able to enjoy, or to excel at, Maths or closely linked subjects such as Physics.

Similar arguments could be made for the need to teach any and every subject from within a Christian context. Whatever the topic is, *'the fear of the LORD is the key to this treasure' (Isa. 33:6)* and *'in Christ lie hidden all the treasures of wisdom and knowledge'* (Col. 2:3).

A radically different view of the child
The schools are further united in their view of the nature of the child. Children are made in the image of God. They belong to him. They are especially important. In Matthew 18, it is recorded that Jesus said, *'Anyone who welcomes a little child like this on my behalf is welcoming me. But if anyone causes one of these little ones who trusts in me to lose faith, it would be better for that person to be thrown into the sea with a large millstone tied around the neck.'* These are strong words, and they affect the Christian schools in two ways. Firstly, they underline the very great challenge and level of responsibility that goes with teaching in a Christian school. On the other hand, they also illustrate exactly why the schools exist and perhaps spell out

one of the reasons why the Lord's presence is felt so strongly in the Christian schools.

The schools also understand that the pupils, be they little ones or teenagers, possess a fallen nature, which explains so much of their behaviour. They know what they are dealing with in this respect. They look to the Bible for guidance on the disciplining of children in a fallen world, but want to exercise that discipline lovingly, to reflect the way in which the heavenly Father deals with all his children.

Common standards

The new schools also share a belief in the high standards of morality that go with a Christian world view, together with a belief in the grace and mercy of God, extended to all of us who grieve because we fail to meet those standards. This is basic Christian doctrine, and it leads to a stable and reassuring framework within which the children can be educated. Far from restricting and stifling children, it does the very opposite by providing a safe environment with clear boundaries within which it is possible for them to flourish – and flourish they do!

More about the past pupils

Young people who have been educated at the new Christian schools generally speaking achieve high academic standards and become successful adults. They tend to be warmly welcomed by sixth form colleges and similar institutions. The reasons given are that they know how to work and they know how to behave. They are assets to the colleges and enrich their community life. In just the same way, employers often express great appreciation of the standards of work and general behaviour of the graduates of the schools.

As the young people progress further through life, many

of them are entering the kind of professions that involve the service of others. A steady stream of teachers, nurses, social workers, church workers, physiotherapists, care workers, university lecturers and so on, is steadily flowing out across Britain from the schools. Others are involved in commerce and industry, seeking to apply Christian principles of honesty and fair-dealing. We believe that the whole of British society is beginning to benefit and some of the young adults have already spent time serving in similar ways overseas.

Common sacrifice

The founding of the schools has required high levels of personal sacrifice and this is something else that is common to them. With no Government funding available, except at nursery level, they are reluctantly part of the private sector but are not elitist and generally speaking do not serve wealthy communities. Teachers work for very low salaries and sometimes for no salary at all. Parents who would not normally be in the market for private education make many sacrifices to raise the necessary fees or work hard within the schools themselves. Ordinary people who would not consider themselves to be pioneers or trail-blazers, capable of great sacrifice, have proved to be just that.

The role of the Trust

As the number of schools has grown, so the work of the Christian Schools' Trust has expanded and developed. It offers advice and support to its member schools by producing publications, arranging conferences, providing teacher-training and stimulating interaction between the schools. It monitors national developments in education and keeps the schools informed of them. It seeks to make both the Government and the churches aware of the existence of the schools and to make visible how successful they are proving to be. The Trust also encourages the founding of new schools, providing assistance to anyone interested in setting one up. Its task is to do all that it can to promote the original aims of the movement, the provision of a distinctively Christian alternative education for those parents and churches who desire such schools for their children.

The Christian Schools' Trust has an increasing role in challenging and training Christian educators, both in the UK and overseas. It has helped to establish and support Christian schools in Africa, Kazakhstan and Poland. Whether in this nation or abroad, it is seeking, under God, to work for the fulfilment of his promise to his people, found in Isaiah 54:13:

All your children will be taught by the LORD, and great will be their peace.

Member Schools
of the Christian Schools' Trust

Kingsland School,
  BANGOR, Northern Ireland 028 9147 3797

Barnsley Christian School,
  BARNSLEY, South Yorkshire 01226 211 011

The King's School,
  BASINGSTOKE, Hampshire 01256 467 092

Bradford Christian School,
  BRADFORD 01274 532 649

Mount Zion School,
  BRISTOL 0117 924 8840

Potters House,
  BURY, Lancashire 0161 705 1885

Folly's End Christian School,
  CROYDON 0208 649 9121

New Life Christian School,
  CROYDON 0208 680 7671

Emmanuel School,
   DERBY 01332 340 505

Gateway Christian School,
   ILKESTON, Derbyshire 01159 440 609

Jubilee House Christian School,
   STANTON, Derbyshire 0115 932 5111

River of Life Christian School,
   DUMFRIES 01387 264 646

Springfield School,
   DUNDEE 01382 500880

King's School Senior,
   EASTLEIGH, Hampshire 02380 600 956

Mannafields Christian School,
   EDINBURGH 0131 659 5602

Regius Christian School,
   EDINBURGH 0131 466 8662

The Cornerstone School,
   EPSOM 01372 742 940

Emmanuel School,
   EXETER 01392 258 150

School of the Lion,
   GLOUCESTER 01452 381 601

The King's School,
   HARPENDEN 01582 767 566

Lewis Independent Christian School,
   ISLE OF LEWIS 01851 700 134

Emmanuel Christian School,
   LEICESTER 0116 222 0792

Christian Fellowship School,
  LIVERPOOL 0151 709 1642

Chrysolyte Independent Christian School,
  LONDON SE1 4XH 0207 407 9990

Dolphin School,
  LONDON SW11 6QP 0207 924 3472

Grangewood Independent School,
  LONDON E7 8QT 0208 472 3552

Thames Christian College,
  LONDON SW11 2HB 0208 241 1382

The King's School,
  NOTTINGHAM 0115 953 9194

Emmanuel Christian School,
  OXFORD 01865 395 236

Plantings School,
  PLYMOUTH 01752 265 171

King's Fold School,
  PRESTON 01772 813 824

Emmanuel Christian School,
  ROCHDALE, Greater Manchester 01706 645 643

The Cedars School,
  ROCHESTER, Kent 01634 847 163

Immanuel School,
  ROMFORD, Essex 01708 764 449

Christ the King School,
  SALE, Cheshire 0161 969 1906

Bethany School,
  SHEFFIELD 0114 272 6994

The King's Primary School,
SOUTHAMPTON 02380 472 266

Trinity School,
STALYBRIDGE, Cheshire 0161 303 0674

Covenant Christian School,
STOCKPORT, Greater Manchester 0161 432 3782

Emmaus School,
TROWBRIDGE, Wiltshire 01225 782 684

Emmanuel School,
WALSALL 01922 635 810

Kingsway School,
WIGAN, Lancashire WN1 3SU 01942 244 743

Winchester Christian Primary School,
WINCHESTER 01962 841 929

The King's School Primary,
WITNEY, Oxfordshire 01993 778 463

The King's School Senior,
WITNEY, Oxfordshire 01993 709 985

River School,
WORCESTER 01905 457 047

The Christian Schools' Trust
Director: Mrs Hilary Reeves
Havering Grange Centre
Havering Road
Romford
RM1 4HR
Tel: 01708 733339
Email: office@christianschoolstrust.co.uk
www.christianschoolstrust.co.uk

The church will never flourish
without Christian schools.
John Calvin

Here is my final conclusion: Fear God and
obey his commands, for this is the duty of
every person. God will judge us for everything
we do, including every secret thing, whether
good or bad (Eccles. 12:13).

Christian Focus Publications

publishes books for all ages

Our mission statement –

STAYING FAITHFUL

In dependence upon God we seek to help make His infallible Word, the Bible, relevant. Our aim is to ensure that the Lord Jesus Christ is presented as the only hope to obtain forgiveness of sin, live a useful life and look forward to heaven with Him.

REACHING OUT

Christ's last command requires us to reach out to our world with His gospel. We seek to help fulfill that by publishing books that point people towards Jesus and help them develop a Christ-like maturity. We aim to equip all levels of readers for life, work, ministry and mission.

Books in our adult range are published in three imprints.

Christian Focus contains popular works including biographies, commentaries, basic doctrine and Christian living. Our children's books are also published in this imprint.

Mentor focuses on books written at a level suitable for Bible College and seminary students, pastors, and other serious readers. The imprint includes commentaries, doctrinal studies, examination of current issues and church history.

Christian Heritage contains classic writings from the past.

Christian Focus Publications, Ltd
Geanies House, Fearn,
Ross-shire, IV20 1TW, Scotland, United Kingdom
info@christianfocus.com

For details of our titles visit us on our website
www.christianfocus.com